INDISPENSABLE REMEDY

INDISPENSABLE REMEDY

The Broad Scope of the Constitution's
Impeachment Power

GENE HEALY

Hardback ISBN: 978-1-948647-36-6
Paperback ISBN: 978-1-948647-35-9
eBook ISBN: 978-1-948647-37-3

Printed in the United States of America.

Library of Congress Cataloging-in-Publication Data available.

Cover design by Jon Meyers.
Interior design by Robert Kern.

Cato Institute
1000 Massachusetts Avenue, N.W.
Washington, D.C. 20001
www.cato.org

Contents

Introduction

Presidential impeachments are rare events in America. In our entire constitutional history, we've seen only three serious attempts to remove a president for "Treason, Bribery, or other high Crimes and Misdemeanors": Andrew Johnson in 1868, Bill Clinton in 1998—both of whom were impeached by the House but escaped removal by the Senate—and Richard Nixon, who resigned in 1974 before the full House could vote.[1] Yet as Donald J. Trump's tumultuous tenure continues, it seems increasingly plausible that we'll see a fourth.

In ordinary times, in ordinary presidencies, the very notion of impeachment is taboo—so near-blasphemous that it comes with its own sanitized euphemism.[2] The "I-Word" is rarely heard during the first year of a new administration, and usually only on the political fringes.[3]

Yet impeachment chatter started on Capitol Hill even before our 45th president was sworn in. On January 9, 2017, 11 days before Trump's inauguration, 24 Democrats, led by Sen. Elizabeth Warren (D-MA), introduced a bill designed to force the incoming president to release his tax returns and put his assets in a blind trust. Should he fail to comply, the Presidential Conflicts of Interest Act stipulated that "it is the sense of Congress that [violation of the act] would constitute a high crime or misdemeanor under Article II, Section 4 of the Constitution of the United States."[4] The next month, Rep. Jerrold Nadler (D-NY) filed a resolution of inquiry demanding that the Justice Department turn over any information in its possession about "President Trump and his associates' conflicts of interest, ethical violations—including the Emoluments Clause—and connections and contacts with Russia."[5] The *Huffington Post* called the move "the first legislative step toward impeachment."[6]

"IMPULSIVE, IGNORANT INCOMPETENCE"

Unsurprisingly, those early warning shots fizzled.[7] But impeachment talk rose from a murmur to a dull roar starting Tuesday, May 9, 2017, when President Trump summarily fired FBI director James Comey. By the end of that week, after Trump admitted in a national television interview that the FBI investigation into "this Russia thing" was a key reason for the termination, the political landscape had changed dramatically. Erstwhile Trump adviser Stephen K. Bannon later called the Comey firing perhaps the biggest mistake in modern political history; it was at least a major self-inflicted wound. The resulting backlash drove Deputy Attorney General Rod Rosenstein to appoint a special counsel, former FBI director Robert Mueller, to oversee the Justice Department's Russia investigation.

June found the president of the United States taking the time to retweet a clip of *Fox & Friends* host Geraldo Rivera pegging the odds of Trump's removal at "0%" and insisting that people "drop that impeachment talk right now!"[8]

Even so, July saw the first article of impeachment formally introduced in the House.[9] Its author, Rep. Brad Sherman (D-CA), limited the charges to obstruction of justice in the Russia investigation, but Sherman's press statement suggested a broader motivation: he described the move as the beginning of "a long process to protect our country from abuse of power, obstruction of justice, and impulsive, ignorant incompetence."[10]

Some of Sherman's colleagues proposed an alternate route toward removal on the basis of incompetence: using the Constitution's Twenty-fifth Amendment to declare the president mentally "unable to discharge the powers and duties of his office."[11] And before that summer's end, two more congressmen threatened to introduce articles of impeachment based on the president's increasingly erratic public conduct. In August 2017, Rep. Steve Cohen (D-TN) proposed impeaching Trump for failed "moral leadership" after the president blamed "both sides" for the violence at a neo-Nazi rally in Charlottesville, Virginia.[12] The next month, Rep. Al Green (D-TX) threatened to bring a floor vote on Trump's impeachment, citing "a level of indecency that is unbecoming [to] the presidency."[13]

By the six-month mark of the administration, support for Trump's impeachment had broken 40 percent in several polls—higher than the president's approval rating at the time,[14] and higher than support for Richard Nixon's impeachment six months into his second term, after he'd refused to hand over the Watergate tapes.[15]

THE DANGERS OF POLITICAL TRIBALISM

Impeachments "will seldom fail to agitate the passions of the whole community, and to divide it into parties," Alexander Hamilton wrote in *Federalist 65*.[16] That's proved to be one of his sounder predictions. The polls on impeaching Trump revealed a wide partisan gap, with as much as a 65-point difference between Democrats and Republicans.[17] And with a Red-Team president now in the dock, prominent players in the Clinton impeachment debate of the late '90s promptly switched sides. "Congress must begin impeachment proceedings immediately," insisted the Democratic activist group MoveOn, named for its inaugural 1998 campaign opposing the Clinton impeachment: "Move On to pressing issues facing the nation," instead.[18] By 2017, though, the group had come around to the view that presidential obstruction of justice was worth lingering over. Meanwhile, the *American Spectator*—the magazine whose investigative reporting on Bill Clinton's sex scandals had helped set impeachment in motion—had developed a serious case of impeachment fatigue.[19] "The times are sour and ill-mannered enough without unnecessary strife over removal of a duly elected president of the United States," William Murchison sniffed at the *Spectator*'s website.[20]

It's easy to understand why so many Americans dismiss impeachment talk as "just politics." The current public debate could easily leave one with that impression. For partisans on both sides, it's verdict first, rationalization afterward; whether impeachment is a vital constitutional safety valve or a "coup against a constitutionally elected president" turns on one's opinion of one Donald J. Trump.[21] Moreover, in a sense, impeachment is *inescapably* political: it's a power, lodged in Congress, designed to remedy serious violations of political trust.

But impeachment isn't *just* political—it's also legal. Contra Gerald Ford, an impeachable offense is *not* "whatever a majority of the House considers it to be at a given moment in history."[22] The Constitution doesn't say simply that the president is removable upon a majority vote in the House and a two-thirds vote in the Senate; Article II, Section 4 provides that the president "shall be removed from Office on Impeachment for, and Conviction of, Treason, Bribery, or other high Crimes and Misdemeanors." Congress is asked to make a legal judgment as well as a political one. And, as citizens, so are we.

In the fog of partisan warfare, we risk getting it wrong. "There will always be the greatest danger that the decision will be regulated more by the comparative strength of parties, than by the real demonstrations of innocence or guilt," Hamilton warned.[23] There's much more at stake than the fate of one particular president, however. Partisans who expand the remedy's scope beyond its constitutional limits, hoping to punish a president they loathe, forge a sword that may someday be used against them. And when their opponents narrow the grounds for removal in the hopes of protecting "their" president, they risk weakening our defenses against future presidents whose behavior gravely threatens the body politic.

The scope of high crimes and misdemeanors is a constitutional question: it shouldn't turn on one's opinion of Donald Trump—we can't afford to let it. The causes of faction may be "sown into the nature of man," but with an issue as vital as this one, it's our responsibility to fight our tribal instincts.[24]

That's no easy task. As the legal scholar Charles Black, Jr. observed in his classic 1974 primer *Impeachment: A Handbook*, impeachment is replete with "questions that have no certain answers. . . . [therefore] it is always tempting to resolve such questions in favor of the immediate political result that is palatable to us . . . to allow one's prejudices to assume the guise of reason."[25]

Approaching the issue as if behind a "veil of ignorance" doesn't seem possible.[26] On the rare occasions that impeachment becomes a live issue, we can't help knowing who's in the crosshairs. But, as Black counseled, we can and should correct for political tribalism through good-faith introspection: by imagining ourselves on the opposite side of the partisan divide from where we now stand, and asking "whether we would have answered the same question the same way" with a different president.[27]

Black urged citizens and legislators alike to approach impeachment from "a stance of principled political neutrality." That's the spirit in which this study will proceed. We'll touch on most of the specific charges lodged against President Trump. But the purpose of this study is not to answer whether Donald Trump should be impeached and removed from office; that question will ultimately be resolved in Congress. Instead, this study is designed to serve as a guide through the history, purpose, and scope of the Constitution's impeachment provisions—and a corrective to some of the popular myths that have grown up around what the Framers considered an "indispensable" remedy.[28]

"THE INCAPACITY, NEGLIGENCE, OR PERFIDY OF THE CHIEF MAGISTRATE"

First among those myths is the notion that impeachment is reserved solely for criminal abuse of power. We tend to think of presidential impeachments in terms of the paradigmatic case: Richard Nixon resigned before he could be impeached, but his case rightfully looms large in the public understanding of "high crimes and misdemeanors."[29] As Cass Sunstein writes in his 2017 book *Impeachment: A Citizen's Guide*, "If a president uses the apparatus of government in an unlawful way, to compromise democratic processes and invade constitutional rights, we come to the heart of what the impeachment provision is all about."[30]

But that's not *all* impeachment is about. During the Philadelphia Convention's most extensive period of debate on the remedy's purpose, James Madison declared it "indispensable that some provision should be made for defending the community against the incapacity, negligence, or perfidy of the Chief Magistrate."[31] The conventional view of the impeachment power collapses everything into the third of those categories: perfidy. But in an office as powerful as the presidency, incapacity and gross negligence can be as dangerous to the country as willful, malicious abuse of power.

In practice, impeachment has never been limited to cases of perfidy alone. In its comprehensive 1974 report, "Constitutional Grounds for Presidential Impeachment," the House Judiciary Committee impeachment inquiry staff identified three categories of misconduct held to be impeachable offenses in American constitutional history: abuse of power, using one's post for personal gain, and "behaving in a manner grossly incompatible with the proper function and purpose of the office." The House has the power to impeach—and the Senate to remove—a federal officer whose conduct "seriously undermine[s] public confidence in his ability to perform his official functions."[32]

Impeachment, Hamilton explained in *Federalist* 65, is designed to reach "those offenses which proceed from the misconduct of public men, or in other words from the abuse or violation of some public trust. They are of a nature which may with peculiar propriety be denominated POLITICAL, as they relate chiefly to injuries done immediately to the society itself."[33] The remedy's scope should therefore be understood in light of its ultimate aim: protection of "the society itself," in Hamilton's words; "defending the community," in Madison's. The end impeachment serves is protection of the body politic; the means it provides are accordingly extensive enough to serve that end. As the 1974 Nixon Inquiry Report put it, impeachment is a remedy designed to "reach a broad variety of conduct by officers that is both serious and incompatible with the duties of the office."[34]

This study begins with a look at impeachment's preconstitutional history: its origins in British practice, more than four centuries before the Philadelphia Convention, and its adoption for revolutionary and republican purposes during the American colonial period. We'll look at how that history informed the constitutionalization of impeachment in the framing and ratification debates. Then we'll survey the American impeachment cases, mining them for insight on the scope and proper application of the remedy.

Readers especially interested in current controversies should feel free to jump ahead to chapter 3, "The Scope of Impeachable Offenses" (page 51). It's there we begin to examine questions that may become especially important in the Trump presidency, such as:

- Do high crimes and misdemeanors require actual violations of the law?
- Can "impulsive, ignorant incompetence" serve as valid grounds for impeachment—or is the Twenty-fifth Amendment, which allows the replacement of a president "unable to discharge the powers and duties of his office," the proper remedy for that sort of presidential incapacity?
- Is it ever constitutionally legitimate to impeach a president for negligence and mismanagement?

- . . . for firing qualified officers or appointing bad ones?
- . . . for failure to adequately staff the executive branch?
- . . . for "private" transgressions, unrelated to the exercise of his office?
- . . . for misconduct that occurred before taking office?
- . . . for misuse of authorities—like the pardon power—the Constitution clearly leaves to the president's discretion?
- . . . for conduct unbecoming the office?

According to conventional wisdom, the answer to most of those questions is "no." As we'll see, however, in most of those cases, the conventional wisdom is wrong. The category of impeachable offenses is much broader than is popularly understood.

Impeachment wasn't meant to be done lightly, but neither were Americans meant to shrink from it when it becomes necessary. As a Cato Institute study published two decades ago, during our last national debate over impeachment, put it: "the winner of a presidential election has only a qualified right to enter and hold the office of the presidency"; if and when the president demonstrates that he or she is unfit for the powers and responsibilities of that office, "Congress has a responsibility to vindicate the Constitution."[35]

1

The Americanization
of Impeachment

By the time of the American Constitutional Convention, impeachments had been used in the mother country for some 400 years. "The model from which the idea of this institution has been borrowed," Hamilton explained in the *Federalist*, was Great Britain, where the practice was understood as "a bridle in the hands of the legislative body upon the executive servants of the government. Is this not the true light in which it ought to be regarded?"[36]

THE ENGLISH MODEL

The practice of parliamentary impeachment began in the 14th century and developed as a means of regulating and punishing men too highly placed to be reachable by ordinary legal means.[37] From the start, the mechanism had a wider ambit than statutory or common law. Some scholars date the first use of the phrase "high Crimes and Misdemeanors" to the 1386 impeachment of the King's Chancellor, Michael de la Pole, Earl of Suffolk.[38] The charges against Suffolk included:

breaking a promise he made to the full Parliament to execute in connection with a parliamentary ordinance the advice of a committee of nine lords regarding the improvement of the estate of the King and the realm; "this was not done, and it was the fault of himself as he was then chief officer."[39]

The 17th-century struggle against Stuart absolutism saw an explosion of impeachments. The mechanism became a key weapon in the fight for parliamentary supremacy and was used to bring the king's ministers to account.[40] In his 1833 *Commentaries on the Constitution*, the American jurist Joseph Story described its broad application: "The parliamentary history of impeachments," Story wrote, included "many offenses, not easily definable by law, and many of a purely political character." He continued:

> Thus, persons have been impeached for giving bad counsel to the king; advising a prejudicial peace; enticing the king to act against the advice of parliament; purchasing offices; preventing other persons from giving counsel to the king, except in their presence; and procuring exorbitant personal grants from the king . . . impeachments for

malversations and neglects in office;
for official oppression, extortions,
and deceits; and especially for putting
good magistrates out of office, and
advancing bad.[41]

The House of Lords operated as a check against the Commons' more ambitious applications of the remedy, often declining to try cases brought before them. Still, the very threat of impeachment—which, under English law, could carry penalties including imprisonment, heavy fines, and even death—provided a powerful incentive against abuse of office. "On many occasions the Commons did not even prosecute," historians Peter Charles Hoffer and N. E. H. Hull note: "the impeachment itself was sufficient warning or inconvenience to the accused."[42]

By 1679, the House of Commons could proclaim impeachment "the chief institution for the preservation of the government."[43] The American colonists viewed the remedy in a similar light, and would adapt it to their own revolutionary and republican purposes.

COLONIAL IMPEACHMENT

The American colonies "were settled during the century of impeachment in England," Hoffer and Hull write, and subsequent developments "gave it a more central role in American constitutionalism than it ultimately had in English law."[44] The last impeachment trial in the House of Lords was held in 1806; as the real power in the English Constitution shifted to Parliament, the Commons developed other methods of oversight and control.[45] Across the Atlantic, however, the colonists embraced the institution, first as a means of disciplining officials appointed by the Crown, and later, as a weapon in the fight against imperial rule.[46]

Technically, colonial assemblies had no legal power to impeach. They did it anyway and persisted even after they were told to stop.[47] From the first colonial impeachment, that of Virginia Governor John Harvey in 1635, to the last, that of Massachusetts Chief Justice Peter Oliver in 1774, on the eve of revolution, the charges tended to sweep broadly. In Harvey's case, they amounted to abuse of power and maladministration, including suppressing petitions to the king and "arrang[ing] a dangerous peace treaty with the Indians."[48] In Oliver's case, the issue was judicial independence: the Massachusetts assembly had vowed to impeach any judge who compromised his impartiality by accepting a royal salary. As Hoffer and Hull note, "Oliver had done nothing averse to English law; indeed, he was impeached for obeying a directive from the crown."[49] But his refusal to renounce the grant led to charges of high crimes and misdemeanors for having acted "against the known Sense of the Body of the People of this Province."[50]

The fact that colonial legislatures had limited power to punish offenders drove some important differences with English practice. English impeachments carried criminal penalties and could even be directed against commoners; in the colonies, impeachment would be employed only against officeholders, whose penalty would be loss of office. "Under the English precedents which guided colonial prosecutions, these deviations were accidents; under republican impeachment law they would become the very heart and soul of the process."[51]

Eight of the original 13 colonies adopted impeachment provisions in their first state constitutions, with three more incorporating the procedure before 1790. Offenses were typically described in expansive terms: "maladministration" was Pennsylvania's sole enumerated offense; New Jersey allowed impeachment for "misbehavior"; New York had "mal and corrupt conduct"; in Delaware, "offending against the state by maladministration, corruption, or other means, by which the safety of the commonwealth may be endangered."[52] The principal method of striking at men in high places would be retained after independence; after all, "There could be no guarantee that republican magistrates in America would escape the temptations that destroyed liberty in England. Human nature, not monarchy, was the root cause of decay."[53]

THE CONSTITUTIONAL CONVENTION DEBATES

When the delegates to the Constitutional Convention assembled in Philadelphia in May 1787, their ranks included men with direct experience in impeachment as advocates, constitutional draftsmen, or litigants, including Virginia's

Edmund Randolph, James Madison, and George Mason; Pennsylvania's James Wilson, Benjamin Franklin, and Gouverneur Morris; and New York's Alexander Hamilton.[54] That experience would help guide them in the debates over three key questions: (1) should the president be removable by impeachment?; (2) if so, by whom?; and (3) on what grounds?

SHOULD THE PRESIDENT BE SUBJECT TO IMPEACHMENT?

A minority of the delegates opposed presidential impeachments altogether: Gouverneur Morris believed that the executive's vulnerability to removal was "a dangerous part of the plan."[55] On July 20, with South Carolina's Charles Pinckney, he moved to strike that provision, arguing that it would "render the Executive dependent on those who are to impeach."[56] That motion sparked the Convention's most extensive discussion of impeachment, with most delegates pronouncing the remedy indispensable. Impeachment was "an essential security for the good behaviour of the Executive," North Carolina's William Davie insisted; a "necessity," James Wilson concurred. "No point is of more importance than that the right of impeachment should be continued," George Mason declared. "Shall any man be above Justice?" he asked, "above all shall that man be above it, who can commit the most extensive injustice?"[57]

As the debate went on, Morris began to back off from his categorical opposition, admitting that "corruption &

some few other offenses to be such as ought to be impeachable." After further objections by Madison, Ben Franklin, Edmund Randolph, and Elbridge Gerry—who "hoped the maxim would never be adopted here that the chief magistrate could do no wrong"—Morris conceded. His "opinion had been changed by the arguments used in the discussion." "This magistrate is not the king, but the prime minister," he affirmed: "The people are the king." On the question "Shall the Executive be removable on impeachments," the delegates voted "yes," eight states to two.[58]

REMOVABLE BY WHOM?

The Virginia Plan, drafted mainly by Madison and introduced by Randolph, made the "National Judiciary" the trial court for impeachments. This was the arrangement Madison favored throughout the Convention. Other proposals included John Dickinson's, which made the executive "removable by the national legislature upon request by a majority of the legislatures of the individual states"; and Hamilton's, for "all impeachments to be tried by a Court to consist of the Chief or Judge of the Superior Court of Law of each state."[59]

In the end, the British system of trial by the upper house appeared the least problematic to the Framers.[60] Morris thought "no other tribunal than the Senate could be trusted. The Supreme Court were too few in number, and might be warped or corrupted," particularly since the president would have a hand in their appointment.[61] On

September 4, the "Committee of Eleven," tasked by the Convention with addressing unresolved issues, recommended designating the Senate as the body for impeachment trials. The Convention approved that proposal, with Virginia and Pennsylvania dissenting.

ON WHAT GROUNDS?

Throughout the Convention, the delegates considered various formulations for the scope of impeachable offenses: "mal-practice or neglect of duty" (June 2); "Mal- and corrupt conduct" (June 18); "Treason, bribery, or corruption" (August 6); and "Neglect of duty, malversation, or corruption" (August 20).[62] Yet by September, the Committee of Eleven had narrowed the grounds for impeachment to "Treason, or bribery." On September 8, the delegates considered that language, prompting an important exchange between Virginia's George Mason and James Madison. "Why is the provision restrained to Treason & bribery only?" Mason asked. Referring to the charges against Warren Hastings, governor-general of India, who had been impeached by the House of Commons weeks before the Constitutional Convention began, Mason objected that "Hastings is not guilty of Treason. Attempts to subvert the Constitution may not be Treason" as defined in the Constitution. He moved to add "or maladministration" after "bribery." Madison countered that "So vague a term will be equivalent to a tenure during the pleasure of the Senate." Mason "withdrew 'maladministration' &

substitute[d] 'other high crimes & misdemeanors agst. the State." The motion passed, eight to three.[63]

THE CONSTITUTIONAL TEXT

"It is striking how often impeachment is mentioned in the Constitution," presidential scholar Jeffrey Tulis observes: "it appears in six clauses and in each of the three articles structuring the major branches of government." Its very prevalence, Tulis suggests, is one indication of the remedy's centrality to a "well-functioning separation of powers regime."[64]

Article I provides that the House "shall have the sole Power of Impeachment," and the Senate, "sole Power to try all Impeachments," with conviction requiring concurrence of two-thirds of the members present.[65] It further limits the penalties that can be imposed by Congress: "Judgment . . . shall not extend further than to removal from Office, and disqualification to hold and enjoy any Office of honor, Trust or Profit under the United States."[66]

Article II, Section 4 defines impeachable offenses: "The President, Vice President and all civil Officers of the United States, shall be removed from Office on Impeachment for, and Conviction of, Treason, Bribery, or other high Crimes and Misdemeanors."

Article II, Section 2 stipulates that the president's otherwise sweeping power to pardon does not extend to cases of impeachment, and, per Article III, Section 2, neither does the right to trial by jury apply to impeachments.

With the passage of time, the key term, "high Crimes and Misdemeanors," has become opaque—even perplexing—to modern readers: "grave felonies, but lesser offenses too?" In U.S. criminal law, "misdemeanor" indicates a minor crime punishable by less than a year in jail. If understood in that sense, Judge Richard Posner has noted that "the constitutional formula would be absurd: either 'high Crimes and low Crimes' or 'high Crimes and high low Crimes.'"[67]

Instead, "misdemeanor" should be understood in a broader sense: "ill behavior; evil conduct; fault; mismanagement," as it's defined in Webster's *American Dictionary of the English Language* (1828).[68] In his *Lectures on Law* (1791), Convention delegate and Supreme Court Justice James Wilson described impeachment as a means of punishing "malversation in office, or what are called high misdemeanors."[69] A misdemeanor in this context indicates "corrupt behavior in a position of trust."[70]

The adjective "high" did not—or did not merely—indicate the seriousness of the offense, but the position of the offender. High crimes and misdemeanors were transgressions committed by men in high places.[71] Thus, William Blackstone's *Commentaries on the Laws of England* lists "high misdemeanors" among offenses against "the king and government," including "embezzling the public money" and "mal-administration of such high offices as are in public trust and employment. This is usually punished by the method of parliamentary impeachment."[72]

"Offenses which proceed from the misconduct of public men," in Hamilton's phrasing, may be too broad to enumerate. By its nature, an impeachment proceeding "can never be tied down by such strict rules . . . as in common cases serve to limit the discretion of courts."[73] As James Wilson put it, impeachments "come not . . . within the sphere of ordinary jurisprudence. They are founded on different principles [and] are governed by different maxims."[74]

Northwestern's John McGinnis has done as good a job as any modern scholar of translating the meaning of high crimes and misdemeanors into contemporary lay language. He argues that the phrase should be understood, roughly, as "objective misconduct that seriously undermines the official's fitness for office . . . measured by the risks, both practical and symbolic, that the officer poses to the republic."[75]

2

The American Impeachment Cases

American impeachment practice reflects that broad under-standing of the remedy's scope. In this section, we'll look at the first impeachments of federal officers in the years after ratification, then turn to our three presidential impeach-ment cases, and close with a look at the cases involving fed-eral judges and other "civil Officers of the United States."

A NOTE ON "PRECEDENT"

As a preliminary matter, however, it's important to appreci-ate the differences between impeachment precedents and those found in judicial caselaw. With impeachment cases, it can often be difficult to discern the "holding." When the House votes to impeach a federal officer, that clearly indi-cates the majority's belief that the officer's conduct rep-resents constitutionally sufficient grounds. But, as the Nixon Inquiry Report observed, "the action of the House in declin-ing to impeach an officer is not particularly illuminating."[76] In any given case, constitutional inadequacy of the charges might play a role, but insufficient proof, political obstacles, or other nonconstitutional factors might be determinative.

Senate refusals to convict present similar interpretive difficulties: we often cannot say with certainty why the charges didn't stick. Individual senators may provide explanations for their votes, but those statements lack the unity and authority of a court's majority opinion. A Senate acquittal can reflect the belief that the accusations were defective as a matter of constitutional law; it can also speak to insufficient evidence (complicated by the fact that there is no official standard of proof) or the judgment, akin to prosecutorial discretion, that even when high crimes and misdemeanors have been committed, removal isn't in the best interests of the political community.[77]

Finally, the doctrine of *stare decisis* has much less force in impeachment practice than in the courts. As the University of Virginia's Michael Klarman observes, "if impeachment is a mixed operation of law and politics, the appropriate role of 'precedent' is uncertain." When Congress declines to pass a law or the Senate declines to ratify a treaty, they don't bind themselves from reconsidering the matter later under different circumstances; so, too, with decisions related to impeachment. And "even courts are free to overturn their own precedents."[78]

For all of those reasons, impeachment decisions by past Congresses are best viewed as "a form of 'persuasive authority.'"[79] They aren't binding precedent, but can serve as useful guideposts for determining the scope of the impeachment power.

IMPEACHMENT IN THE EARLY REPUBLIC

Arguably, *early* practice, contemporaneous with the generation that ratified the Constitution, should be considered especially persuasive. The University of Chicago's David Currie, author of the four-volume history *The Constitution in Congress*, notes that the early Congresses functioned as a "sort of continuing constitutional convention," in which the members, many of whom had helped draft or ratify the document, interpreted its provisions in the process of applying them.[80] The first decade and a half under the new Constitution saw the first three impeachments of federal officers, to which we now turn.

Senator William Blount (1797–1799)

The first federal impeachment case was also the only occasion on which impeachment has been deployed against a member of Congress. William Blount, former territorial governor of Tennessee, became a senator upon the state's admission to the Union in 1796. A heavily overextended land speculator, Blount's investments depended on Western access to the Mississippi River. To ensure that access, Blount hatched a plan to invade Spanish-held Florida and Louisiana territory with a private army of frontiersmen and Cherokee and Creek Indians, backed by the British. Blount's correspondence with an Indian interpreter he sought to enlist in the plot made its way to the desk of President John Adams, who forwarded it to the Senate and the House.[81] Blount walked into the Senate chamber on July

3, 1797, just as his letter was being read—and skipped town shortly thereafter.

A Senate committee found Blount "guilty of a high misdemeanor, entirely inconsistent with his public trust and duty as a Senator," and he was promptly expelled from the upper house.[82] Meanwhile, the House of Representatives proceeded to impeach him.

The first article of impeachment charged that Blount had contrived "to create, promote, and set on foot . . . a military hostile expedition" against Spain, "contrary to the duty of his trust and station as a Senator of the United States, in violation of the obligations of neutrality, and against the laws of the United States, and the peace and interests thereof."[83] The articles alluded to violations of U.S. law, yet, as Jonathan Turley notes, "the Senate trial did not emphasize such alleged criminal acts as opposed to the view that the conduct was simply contemptible and outrageous for any public figure."[84]

Blount's lawyers made three arguments in his defense: first, that senators weren't "civil Officers of the United States" under Article II, Section 4 of the Constitution; second, that having already been stripped of his office, Blount was now a private citizen and couldn't be convicted; and third, that his acts did not amount to high crimes and misdemeanors. The defense put most of the weight on the claim that senators weren't impeachable, and that's likely what carried the day. "The public record does not reveal how many Senators were persuaded by each of [the] three arguments," Currie explains, but "the acknowledged weakness of two of them may lead us to surmise that the dominant conclusion was that members of Congress are not 'officers of the United States.'"[85] The Senate, by a vote of 14–11, refused jurisdiction of the case.[86]

Judge John Pickering (1803–1804)

The next two impeachment efforts were directed at the judicial branch and reflected Jeffersonian efforts to tame the Federalist-packed federal courts. The Judiciary Act of 1801, passed by the lame-duck Federalist Congress after the overwhelming Democratic-Republican victory in the 1800 election, stacked the judiciary for the Federalists, creating 16 new circuit court judges. "They have retired into the Judiciary as a stronghold," Jefferson complained, "and from that battery all the works of republicanism are to be beaten down and erased."[87] One response was to attack the expansion directly, which Jefferson's congressional allies did by repealing the 1801 act. The second was to target the worst offenders among Federalist judges for impeachment.[88]

"The enclosed letter and affidavits," Jefferson wrote to the House in February 1803, "exhibiting matter of complaint against John Pickering, district judge of New Hampshire, [are] not within executive cognizance," but "the Constitution has confided [in the House] a power of instituting proceedings of redress."[89] The implication was clear.

According to the articles of impeachment approved by the House in early 1804, Pickering had revealed himself to be a man "of loose morals and intemperate habits," guilty of "high misdemeanors, disgraceful to his own character as a judge." The immediate cause was the judge's handling of an admiralty case: the first three articles charged him with various legal errors and arbitrary rulings involving a ship seized for violation of customs duties.[90] The fourth article accused Pickering, essentially, of conduct unbecoming his office. The judge had appeared in court "in a state of total intoxication, produced by the free and intemperate use of intoxicating liquors" and behaved in a "profane and indecent manner . . . degrading to the honor of the United States."[91]

Although the articles don't state it in so many words, Pickering's problems went beyond a fondness for drink. The judge's own son confirmed that his father was "altogether incapable of transacting any kind of business which requires the exercise of judgment, or the faculties of reason," and the Senate heard evidence from two of the judge's doctors to the effect that he'd gone insane.

The idea of impeaching an officer who wasn't in his right mind was controversial.[92] Pickering's Federalist defenders called it an absurdity, and some Republican senators shared those qualms.[93] Even so, the Senate removed Pickering on March 12, 1804. As Pennsylvania's Sen. George Logan put it: "If the Judge is insane, whether it be by *the act of God* or his *own imprudence*, is immaterial—for in either case he is incapable of discharging the duties of Judge."[94]

Justice Samuel Chase (1804–1805)

The same day the Senate convicted Pickering, the House impeached Supreme Court Justice Samuel Chase. The triggering offense here was a partisan diatribe Chase had unleashed on a Baltimore grand jury while riding circuit in 1803. Chase assailed the repeal of the 1801 Judiciary Act, attacked universal suffrage—which would cause the country's descent into "mobocracy"—and took aim at the very principles of the Declaration of Independence: insisting that the "modern doctrines by our late reformers, that all men in a state of society are entitled to enjoy equal liberty and equal rights, have brought this mighty mischief upon us; and I fear that it will rapidly progress until peace and order, freedom and property, shall be destroyed." Upon reading a newspaper report about the justice's rant, Jefferson wrote to a congressional ally, asking "to whom so pointedly as yourself will the public look for the necessary measures," to remedy this attack on "the principles of our Constitution?" "For myself," the president closed, "it is better than I should not interfere." (Jefferson, Henry Adams writes, "was somewhat apt to say that it was better he should not interfere in the same breath with which he interfered.")[95]

The eight articles of impeachment approved by the House in 1804 weren't based on Chase's speech alone; they also charged him with rank pro-prosecution bias against Republican defendants in several trials conducted while the justice was riding circuit. Chase had barred defense counsel in a treason trial from addressing the jury on the law; in a Sedition Act trial, he'd seated a juror who'd already concluded the defendant was guilty; and had, per Article VII, "descend[ed] from the dignity of a judge and stoop[ed] to the level of an informer" by pressuring a Delaware grand jury to investigate a printer for sedition. Only the eighth article covered the Baltimore grand jury incident, claiming that Chase "did . . . pervert his official right and duty to address the grand jury" by delivering "an intemperate and inflammatory political harangue," and engaging in conduct "highly censurable in any, but peculiarly indecent and unbecoming" in a Justice of the Supreme Court. Chase was acquitted on all charges, but came closest to conviction on Article VIII, based on the "inflammatory political harangue": the vote, 19–15, was four short of the necessary two-thirds.[96]

The Senate's failure to convict marked the end of Republican efforts to reshape the courts via impeachment. "Experience has already shown," Jefferson would later complain, that "the impeachment [the Constitution] has provided is not even a scarecrow."[97] That assessment was likely too bleak: the threat of impeachment had a pronounced effect on Chase's subsequent behavior, and "from that moment until his death," historian Gordon Wood writes, "he ceased engaging in political controversy."[98] Other judges took a similar lesson, helping foster a new norm against blatant partisanship from the bench.[99]

PRESIDENTIAL IMPEACHMENTS

Jefferson's "scarecrow" comment might have been closer to the mark if applied to our paltry record of presidential impeachments. Of our 44 presidents, so far only three have faced a genuine threat of removal via impeachment. Only two were actually impeached, and neither was removed by the Senate. All three cases bear close scrutiny.

Andrew Johnson (1868)

The first president to be impeached, and the one who came closest to conviction in the Senate, was Andrew Johnson. The only senator from a Confederate state to stick with the Union, Johnson's ardent opposition to secession led to his appointment by President Lincoln as military governor of Tennessee in 1862. In 1864, seeking to balance the ticket with a War Democrat, the Republicans replaced Lincoln's first-term running mate, Maine's Hannibal Hamlin, with Johnson under the rebranded "National Union Party" ticket. Like John Tyler, Johnson would become an "accidental president": six weeks after inauguration, Lincoln's assassination would deliver him to the presidency.

Johnson soon came into conflict with the Radical Republicans over the direction and severity of Reconstruction. On May 29, 1865, he issued two proclamations signaling his intent to reform Southern state governments without Congress.[100] The first granted amnesty to most ex-Confederates, restoring their voting rights conditional on swearing a loyalty oath to the Union; the second outlined a plan for North Carolina's readmission to the Union on lenient terms.[101] By the time Congress met in December 1865, Johnson had established provisional governments in 8 of 11 former Confederate states, which had enacted stringent restrictions on the rights of the freedmen and elected, according to an 1866 congressional report, "notorious and unpardoned rebels, men who could not take the prescribed oath of office, and who made no secret of their hostility to the government and the people of the United States."[102]

It trivializes Johnson's impeachment to characterize it as rooted in mere policy differences. "The Johnson impeachment was centrally about presidential power," Princeton's Keith Whittington writes.[103] Johnson used his pardon, veto, and commander-in-chief authorities aggressively, aiming to seize control of Reconstruction. As the historian Michael Les Benedict explains, "Republicans approached impeachment reluctantly, unwillingly, and only voted for impeachment after they were convinced that the president had violated the law and intended to abort congressional authority over Reconstruction by any means necessary."[104]

Initial efforts to impeach Johnson failed for lack of support among moderate Republicans.[105] But in 1867, Congress set a trap for the president in the form of the Tenure of Office Act. The law, passed by overriding Johnson's veto, struck at the president's power to remove executive branch officials. It stipulated that federal officers appointed with the advice and consent of the Senate would retain their posts until the Senate had confirmed a successor, and that cabinet officers could not be removed without the Senate's consent.[106] It further specified that violations of its terms would constitute an impeachable "high misdemeanor."[107]

Johnson took the bait the following year. In February 1868, he fired Secretary of War Edwin M. Stanton, the Radical Republicans' key ally in the administration, who had worked to undermine Johnson's Reconstruction policies.[108] Three days later, the House impeached the president by an overwhelming margin of 126–47. Nine of the 11 articles forwarded by the House were based on violations of the Tenure of Office Act.

"The articles were a jumbled horror," David O. Stewart writes in his history of the Johnson impeachment. "Having failed a few months before with broad and amorphous impeachment allegations, the impeachers had careened to the other extreme, keeping their focus painfully narrow and obscurely legalistic." They charged "the man who betrayed the sacrifice of Union soldiers while abandoning the freed slaves to lives of want and oppression—with misapplying a personnel statute."[109]

The Tenth Article of impeachment, brainchild of former Union general and lead impeachment manager Rep. Benjamin Butler (R-MA), took a different approach. It rested neither on violations of the law nor abuses of power, but on a series of "inflammatory and scandalous" speeches the president had given in his "Swing around the Circle" tour, undertaken to rally support for his policies before the 1866 midterm elections. In those speeches, Johnson,

> unmindful of the high duties of his high office and the dignity and proprieties thereof. . . . did attempt to bring into disgrace, ridicule, hatred, contempt and reproach, the Congress of the United States, [and did] make and declare, with a loud voice, certain intemperate, inflammatory and scandalous harangues, and therein utter loud threats and bitter menaces, as well against Congress as the laws of the United States duly enacted thereby, amid the cries, jeers and laughter of the multitudes then assembled in hearing. . . .
>
> Which said utterances, declarations, threats and harangues, highly censurable in any, are peculiarly indecent and unbecoming in the Chief Magistrate of the United States, by means whereof the said Andrew Johnson has brought the high office of the President of the United States into contempt, ridicule and disgrace, to the great scandal of all good citizens, whereby said Andrew

Johnson, President of the United States,
did commit, and was then and there
guilty of a high misdemeanor in office.[110]

Article X quotes the offending speeches at length. In Cleveland, Johnson had accused Congress of fomenting disunion and "undertak[ing] to poison the minds of the American people," and at a stop in St. Louis, Johnson blamed Congress for a massacre of freedmen that had taken place in New Orleans in July:

> If you will take up the riot at New
> Orleans and trace it back to the Radical
> Congress, you will find that the riot
> at New Orleans was substantially
> planned. . . . every drop of blood that
> was shed is upon their skirts and they
> are responsible.[111]

Article X never came to a vote, having been abandoned after failure to convict on other articles. The Senate voted first on the final article of impeachment, which the Republicans believed to have the strongest support. It failed by one vote. The Senate then adjourned for 10 days, during which time the GOP Convention in Chicago nominated Ulysses S. Grant for president. When the senators returned, they took up the second and third articles, both of which failed by the same margin. Recognizing that the remainder of the charges would meet a similar fate, the Senate adjourned.

Politics is never wholly absent from impeachment proceedings, but in Johnson's case political factors loomed even larger than usual. Under the presidential succession law then in effect, Johnson's replacement would have been the president pro tempore of the Senate, Ohio's Ben Wade. The specter of Wade as president, a Republican too radical for moderate sensibilities, likely swayed more than a few votes. Moreover, as former Chief Justice William H. Rehnquist observed in his 1992 book *Grand Inquests*, "Johnson seemed less a menace in May 1868" than he had in February. He had only 10 months left in office; he had promised privately to appoint a confirmable successor to Stanton, and he wasn't going to be the nominee for either party.[112] Bribery of key senators, suspected but not proven, may also have played a role in Johnson's acquittal.[113]

But the weakness of the charges was clearly a key factor. Johnson's attorneys had argued that Stanton wasn't covered by the terms of the act; that even if he were, its applicability wasn't clear enough to justify removal and the act itself was unconstitutional. Five of the seven "Republican recusants" who'd crossed the aisle to vote for acquittal made public statements explaining their votes, with several echoing those arguments.[114]

The Republicans had overreached. It would be more than a century before there would be another meaningful attempt to impeach a president.

Richard Nixon

"I brought myself down," over Watergate, Richard Nixon lamented in 1977. Self-pitying even when confessing error, he told interviewer David Frost, "I gave them a sword, and they stuck it in and twisted it with relish."[115]

The chain of events leading to that self-inflicted wound began with the creation of the White House "Plumbers" in the summer of 1971. After former Defense Department analyst Daniel Ellsberg began leaking portions of the "Pentagon Papers," a classified DoD history of the Vietnam War, Nixon told his attorney general: "We've got to get this son of a bitch."[116] The Plumbers, led by ex-CIA operative E. Howard Hunt and former FBI agent G. Gordon Liddy, warmed up by breaking into the office of Lewis Fielding, Ellsberg's psychiatrist, hoping to find leakable dirt on the leaker. Then on June 17, 1972, the Plumbers got caught in the act, attempting to repair phone taps they'd installed at Democratic National Committee headquarters in the Watergate office complex. Over the next two years, the story behind the break-in gradually emerged from the courts, congressional hearings, and the press.

The Senate Watergate Committee had unearthed the existence of the White House taping system in July 1973, and special prosecutor Archibald Cox issued a subpoena seeking the tapes. In October, when Cox refused Nixon's "compromise" offer of edited transcripts, Nixon ordered his firing. The "Saturday Night Massacre" proved to be a turning point: the first time a plurality of Americans polled supported the president's removal.[117] When Cox's replacement, Leon Jaworski, renewed the demand for the tapes, Nixon refused, claiming an absolute, unqualified privilege to withhold presidential communications. On July 24, 1974, a unanimous Supreme Court rejected Nixon's claim, holding that the demonstrated need for evidence in the criminal trial outweighed the president's interest in confidentiality.[118]

Three days after the Court's ruling in *United States v. Nixon*, the House Judiciary Committee approved the first article of impeachment by a vote of 27 to 11. Article I charged the president with obstruction of justice in connection with the FBI, special prosecutor, and congressional committees' investigation of the Watergate burglary. Nixon had misled investigators, withheld evidence, suborned perjury, approved "hush money" payments to Watergate defendants, and lied to the American people about his own involvement in the scheme, "making or causing to be made false or misleading public statements for the purpose of deceiving the people of the United States into believing that a thorough and complete investigation had been conducted." "In all of this," Article I concluded, "Richard M. Nixon has acted in a manner contrary to his trust as President and subversive of constitutional government, to the great prejudice of the cause of law and justice and to the manifest injury of the people of the United States."[119]

The Judiciary Committee approved the second article of impeachment two days later, by a vote of 28–10. Its thrust was abuse of executive power. Nixon, Article II charged, had:

> repeatedly engaged in conduct violating
> the constitutional rights of citizens,
> impairing the due and proper admin-
> istration of justice and the conduct of
> lawful inquiries, or contravening the
> laws governing agencies of the execu-
> tive branch and the purposes of these
> agencies.[120]

Among other offenses, the president had sought to have his political enemies audited by the Internal Revenue Service; ordered FBI wiretaps for political purposes "unrelated to any lawful function of his office"; authorized "a secret investigative unit" (the Plumbers) to engage in "covert and unlawful activities," including the burglary of Fielding's office; and "knowingly misused the executive power by interfering with agencies of the executive branch," including the FBI and the CIA.[121]

The final article of impeachment, passed the next day by a narrower margin of 21–17, accused the president of having "failed without lawful cause or excuse to produce papers and things as directed by duly authorized subpoenas" issued by the Judiciary Committee, "thereby assuming to himself functions and judgments necessary to the exercise of the sole power of impeachment vested by the Constitution in the House of Representatives."[122] In other words, Nixon's resistance to lawful demands for evidence in an impeachment inquiry was *itself* grounds for impeachment.

Two more articles considered by the Committee failed to advance to the full House. An "Article on Emoluments and Tax Evasion" charged that Nixon had "unlawfully received compensation in the form of government expenditures" for renovations at two of his private residences and claimed more than half a million dollars in tax deductions to which he was not legally entitled.[123] Another was based on the secret bombing of Cambodia in 1969–1970, which had been deliberately concealed from Congress in derogation of its power to declare war.[124] Both articles failed by votes of 12–26.

On August 5, 1974, Nixon finally surrendered the so-called smoking-gun tape he'd kept hidden even from his own lawyers. Recorded six days after the break-in at Democratic National Committee headquarters, it revealed the president scheming to get the CIA to quash the FBI investigation—making it clear that Nixon was in on the cover-up from the start.[125] With the full House poised to vote for impeachment, and his support in the Senate evaporating, Nixon would resign the presidency by the week's end.

Bill Clinton

John Wayne, a diehard Nixon supporter, once dismissed Watergate as a "damned panty raid."[126] The pivotal moment leading to the Clinton impeachment was the flash of a 22-year-old intern's thong. Monica Lewinsky's invitation, issued in the midst of the 1995 government shutdown, proved irresistible to the president. That lapse in self-restraint would cost Clinton dearly when evidence of the affair—and his efforts to cover it up—fell into the hands of Independent Counsel Kenneth Starr.

In August 1994, after President Clinton signed a reauthorization of the post-Watergate Independent Counsel statute, Starr took over the investigation into the Whitewater affair, a failed real-estate venture the Clintons had entered into in 1978. With permission from the attorney general and the judicial oversight panel set up by the statute, Starr eventually expanded his probe into the firing of White House Travel Office personnel, misuse of FBI files by White House aides, and a host of other matters.[127] Meanwhile, lawyers for former Arkansas state employee Paula Jones, who'd brought a sexual harassment suit against Clinton, sought testimony from Lewinsky.[128]

Lewinsky's coworker and confidante Linda Tripp, who had secretly recorded her conversations with Lewinsky about the affair, approached Starr's team in January 1998. Starr secured permission to investigate obstruction of justice in the Jones case. By August, he'd amassed ample evidence for the charge. The smoking gun in the Clinton case was a stained dress, turned over by Lewinsky under threat of prosecution for perjury in the Jones case.[129]

The Independent Counsel statute required Starr to "advise the House of Representatives of any substantial and credible information . . . that may constitute grounds for an impeachment," and the GOP House leadership spent the summer and fall of 1998 eagerly awaiting Starr's bill of particulars.[130] It would, House Speaker Newt Gingrich (R-GA) thought, "be heavy-laden with non-Lewinsky impeachable offenses," including "Chinese missile technology transfers, the Teamsters money laundering, campaign finance irregularities, etc."[131] "We are going to get a report from Ken Starr, and it will be a masterpiece," Judiciary Committee chairman Henry Hyde (R-IL) told his colleagues in June.[132] Instead, they got 445 pages related to the Lewinsky cover-up, and went to political war with the charges they had.

On December 19, 1998, the House approved two articles of impeachment. The first, passed by a vote of 228–206, charged Clinton with perjury before a federal grand jury. He'd given false and misleading testimony about the nature of his relationship with "a subordinate Government employee" (Lewinsky) and regarding the truthfulness of his prior testimony in the Jones lawsuit and his efforts to mislead the court in that case.[133]

Article II, passed by a 221–212 vote, charged the president with obstruction of justice in the Jones case and the federal grand jury proceeding. According to Article II, Clinton had encouraged Monica Lewinsky to file a false affidavit about their relationship, attempted to get her a job to ensure her cooperation, and "made false and misleading statements to [other] potential witnesses" in the hopes of influencing their testimony. Such actions "undermined the integrity of his office" and subverted "the rule of law and justice, to the manifest injury of the people of the United States."[134]

The House considered, and rejected, two additional articles: one based on "Perjury in the Civil Case" and another on "Abuse of Power." The former covered the president's false testimony in the Jones case; the latter, based on Nixon Article III, charged that by giving false, misleading, and incomplete responses during the impeachment inquiry, Clinton had "assumed to himself functions and judgments necessary to the exercise of the sole power of impeachment" invested in the House. Both failed to pass, the latter by a wide margin.[135]

When the House Republicans set the Clinton impeachment in motion in October 1998 they faced a president with a 67 percent approval rating and a public firmly opposed to his removal.[136] In the congressional elections the next month, the president's party picked up House seats, the first time that had happened in a midterm election since the New Deal.[137] It was a lame-duck House that passed the two articles of impeachment on December 19, 1998. The Senate trial, which began in January, was a foregone conclusion. On February 9, 1999 the Senate voted to acquit on Article I (perjury before the grand jury), 45–55, and Article II (obstruction), 50–50.

OTHER "CIVIL OFFICERS OF THE UNITED STATES"

Of the 19 impeachments approved by the House since the Constitution's ratification, only two have involved presidents.[138] Most of American impeachment practice has involved the other "civil Officers of the United States" referenced in Article II, Section 4.

Only one Cabinet officer has ever been impeached: Gilded Age Secretary of War William Belknap (1876), whom the House charged with "basely prostituting his high office to his lust for private gain" by taking bribes and kickbacks in connection with an appointment to a military trading post. Belknap, who'd resigned just before the House vote, argued that a Senate trial was superfluous, since private citizens weren't subject to impeachment. The Senate proceeded to trial anyway, but failed to convict, in part because many of those voting not guilty believed they lacked jurisdiction.[139]

The overwhelming majority of federal impeachment cases—15 of the 19 approved by the House, and 13 of 16 Senate trials—have targeted federal judges.[140] On the eve of the Nixon impeachment inquiry, Raoul Berger noted that the remedy Parliament had once hailed as "the chief institution for the preservation of the government" had become for Americans "largely a means for the ouster of corrupt judges."[141]

Still, the judicial impeachment cases are instructive: they show that, in American practice, "high Crimes and Misdemeanors" has been understood to cover a wide

variety of "misconduct incompatible with the official position of the officeholder," as the Nixon Inquiry Report put
it.[142] Returning to the three categories of impeachable misconduct outlined in that report, we find numerous examples of each among the judges the House has impeached.

"Improper Purpose or Personal Gain"

Corruption, petty or otherwise, features heavily in the
judicial impeachment cases. The Nixon Inquiry Report
lists the impeachments of district court judges Charles
Swayne (1904), Robert Archbald (1912), Harold Louderback
(1932), and Halsted Ritter (1936) as involving the "use of
office for direct or indirect personal monetary gain."[143] The
post-Watergate cases present similar issues, with district
court judges Alcee Hastings (solicitation of bribery) and
Walter Nixon (perjury before a grand jury) removed by the
Senate in 1989 and Judge G. Thomas Porteous convicted in
2010 for a pattern of corrupt conduct including kickbacks
from lawyers appearing before him.[144]

"Exceeding the Constitutional Bounds of the Powers of the Office"

Other judicial impeachments, starting with the 1805 trial
of Justice Chase, have involved classic abuse-of-power
concerns. Among the charges against Chase were evidentiary rulings showing pro-prosecution bias and denying the
defendant his Sixth Amendment rights in a treason trial. In
1830, the House impeached district judge James Peck for

abusing his contempt powers by imprisoning and suspending an attorney who'd published an article criticizing one of Peck's decisions. The charges against Judge Swayne (1904) included imprisoning and fining attorneys "without authority of law." (In both cases, the Senate failed to convict.)[145]

Conduct "Grossly Incompatible with the Proper Function and Purpose of the Office"

A number of the judicial impeachment cases, including those of the first two judges impeached by the House, include misconduct that doesn't fit neatly under either corruption or abuse of power, but which Congress simply considered beyond the pale. Justice Chase escaped removal, but the vote came closest on the article charging him with haranguing a grand jury in the tones of "an electioneering partisan."[146] And, as noted earlier, district judge John Pickering was impeached and removed mainly for showing up to work drunk and ranting maniacally in court.

The 1873 case of Mark H. Delahay involved another federal judge with "loose morals and intemperate habits" related to the bottle. Rep. Benjamin Butler, who'd earlier played a key role in the impeachment of President Johnson, summed up the case against Delahay as follows:

> The most grievous charge, and that
> which is beyond all question, was that
> his personal habits unfitted him for the
> judicial office; that he was intoxicated

off the bench as well as on the bench. This question has also been decided by precedent. That was the exact charge against Judge Pickering, of New Hampshire.

The committee agree that there is enough in [Delahay's] personal habits to found a charge upon, and that is all there is in this resolution.[147]

Much more recently, in 2009, the House impeached Judge Samuel B. Kent of the Southern District of Texas for repeatedly groping two court employees. Although the year before a federal grand jury had indicted Judge Kent on charges of abusive sexual conduct and obstruction of justice, the House emphasized the disgrace he'd brought to his office rather than his violations of federal law.[148]

Repeatedly in the judicial impeachment cases, the articles include charges that the judge's conduct undermined confidence in the impartiality of the court, which by itself constitutes a high crime or misdemeanor. Judge George W. English, impeached in 1926, had exhibited bizarre behavior suggesting mental unfitness for office: summoning several state and local officials to appear before him "in an imaginary case" and haranguing them "in a loud, angry voice, using improper profane and indecent language."[149] In 1936, the Senate acquitted Judge Halsted Ritter on articles charging kickbacks and income-tax evasion, but voted to convict on a catch-all article charging that his conduct had degraded his office. The articles in the English and Ritter cases employ similar language, to the effect that the officer's conduct brought his court into "scandal and disrepute," undermining public confidence in the administration of justice.[150]

Judges, Presidents, and Precedents

If a federal judge can be impeached for degrading his court, does that mean a president can be impeached for undermining public confidence in the professionalism, competence, and sound judgment of the executive branch? The answer to that question depends on the relevance of judicial impeachment precedents to cases involving the president.

During the fight over the Clinton impeachment, the president's defenders argued that a different constitutional standard applied: removing the federal government's chief executive officer should be harder than removing one of several hundred federal judges. After all, they pointed out, where judges serve for life, presidents have limited tenure, and can be denied a second term by the voters. Further, Article III, Section 1, provides that judges "shall hold their Offices during good Behavior," which arguably implies a lower bar to impeachment and removal.[151] Finally, given the presidency's expansive role in American governance, "it is uniquely destabilizing if presidents are too freely subject to removal from office."[152] As Yale's Akhil Amar puts it:

When a lower federal judge or cabinet head is impeached and removed, the nation undergoes no great trauma. No federal judge or cabinet secretary has a personal mandate from the national electorate, and so her removal does not undo the votes of millions.[153]

None of those distinctions makes out a compelling constitutional argument for special leniency toward presidents. First, the constitutional grounds for impeachment set out in Article II, Section 4—"Treason, Bribery, or other high Crimes and Misdemeanors"—apply to "all civil Officers of the United States" without qualification. The purpose of the "good behavior" clause was not to establish a separate standard for impeaching judges but "simply to make clear that judges ordinarily have life tenure."[154]

Second, although removing a president via the impeachment process is more disruptive than removing one of hundreds of federal judges, it's hardly an assault on democratic principles. Contra Professor Amar, it does not "undo the votes of millions" to replace a duly elected president with his hand-picked, *also* duly elected, running mate.

Third, the argument that presidents are singularly important cuts both ways. While we suffer "no great trauma" from removing an unfit federal judge, we also run no great risk if we hesitate. Judges don't supervise the entire federal law enforcement apparatus or have the massive destructive capacity of the U.S. military at their disposal. Given the damage an unfit president can do, it can be "uniquely destabilizing" to retain one in office.

3

The Scope of
Impeachable Offenses

The American impeachment cases reflect the remedy's application to a wide variety of misconduct. Federal officers have been impeached for abuse of official power, but also for petty corruption, arbitrary judicial rulings, drunkenness and gross incompetence, withholding information from Congress, and degrading their high offices—whether or not those offenses happened to violate the law. And yet, in our current debate over impeachment, even the president's opponents take a narrow, legalistic view of impeachable offenses. Thus, House minority leader Nancy Pelosi (D-CA) has dismissed calls for Trump's impeachment, insisting that "when and if he breaks the law, that is when something like that would come up."[155]

YOU DON'T HAVE TO BREAK THE
LAW TO BE IMPEACHED

That's the wrong standard. Even if, to borrow a phrase from former FBI director James Comey, "no reasonable prosecutor" would bring a criminal charge against the president, that wouldn't mean impeachment is off-limits. Impeachable offenses aren't limited to crimes.

Had the Framers restricted impeachment to statutory offenses, they'd have rendered the power a "complete nullity" from the start, as Justice Joseph Story noted in 1833.[156] In the early republic, there were very few federal crimes, and certainly not enough to cover the range of misdeeds that would rightly disqualify public officials from continued service.[157] Story observed that, in the impeachment cases since ratification, "no one of the charges has rested upon any statutable misdemeanours."[158] In fact, as a Congressional Research Service report explained in 2015, over our entire constitutional history, fewer than a third of the impeachments approved by the House "have specifically invoked a criminal statute or used the term 'crime.'"[159]

That actual crimes are not a prerequisite for impeachment is a settled point among constitutional scholars. Even those who take a restrictive view of the scope of high crimes and misdemeanors, such as Cass Sunstein, recognize that "an impeachable offense, to qualify as such, need not be a crime."[160] Michael Gerhardt sums up the academic consensus: "The major disagreement is not over whether impeachable offenses should be strictly limited to indictable crimes, but rather over the range of nonindictable offenses on which an impeachment may be based."[161]

The impeachment process and the criminal law serve distinct purposes and have very different consequences.[162] The criminal law is designed to punish and deter, but those goals are secondary to impeachment, which aims at removing federal officers unfit for continued service. And where the criminal law deprives the convicted party of liberty, the constitutional penalties for impeachable offenses "shall not extend further than to removal from Office" and possible disqualification from future officeholding.[163] As Justice Story explained, the remedy "is not so much designed to punish an offender, as to secure the state against gross official misdemeanors. It touches neither his person, nor his property; but simply divests him of his political capacity."[164]

No doubt being ejected from a position of power on the grounds that you're no longer worthy of the public's trust can *feel* like a punishment. But the mere fact that removal is stigmatizing doesn't suggest that criminal law standards apply. Raoul Berger once illustrated that point with an analogy Donald Trump would probably find insulting: "to the extent that impeachment retains a residual punitive aura, it may be compared to deportation, which is attended by very painful consequences, but which, the Supreme Court held, 'is not a punishment for a crime.'"[165]

"SUBSTANTIALITY" AND THE LIMITS OF LAW

Madison's tripartite classification of presidential threats, "incapacity, negligence, [and] perfidy," is instructive here. All three categories describe dangers to the body politic, but only one of them—"perfidy," a word with connotations of "wickedness," "treachery," and "breach of faith"—clearly evokes criminal culpability.[166]

Because impeachment's ultimate aim is defense of the political community, in practice "the emphasis has been on the significant effects of the conduct—undermining the integrity of office, disregard of constitutional duties and oath of office, arrogation of power, abuse of the governmental process, adverse impact on the system of government." Moreover, as the Nixon Inquiry Report explains, "not all presidential misconduct is sufficient to constitute grounds for impeachment. There is a further requirement—substantiality." Impeachment should "be predicated only upon conduct seriously incompatible with either the constitutional form and principles of our government or the proper performance of constitutional duties of the presidential office."[167]

Here we come up against the limits of legal analysis: the tools of constitutional interpretation can tell us, for example, that obstruction of justice is, in principle, an impeachable offense. They cannot tell us whether a particular case of presidential obstruction represents an intolerable violation of the public trust, one that demands the president's removal from office. "The answer, when answer must be given, must probably be to some extent political," Charles Black writes, "law can lead us to the point where 'substantiality' becomes the issue, but law cannot tell us what is 'substantial' for the purpose of decision."[168]

With that qualification in mind, for the remainder of this study, we'll explore the contours of the impeachment power in each of Madison's three categories, starting with its applicability to cases of presidential "incapacity."

4

Incapacity and Incompetence

When he introduced the first article of impeachment against President Trump in July 2017, Rep. Brad Sherman suggested that the real problem with the president was that he was incapable of doing the job. "Every day," Sherman complained, "Democrats, Republicans, and the entire world are shocked by the latest example of America's amateur President. Ignorance accompanied by a refusal to learn. Lack of impulse control, accompanied by a refusal to have his staff control his impulses." Still, Sherman said, he'd felt compelled to base the article on obstruction of justice because "the Constitution does not provide for the removal of a President for impulsive, ignorant incompetence."[169]

When it comes to the "most powerful office in the world," however, impulsive, ignorant incompetence can be as damaging as willful criminality. Did the Framers really leave us defenseless against it?

Actually, no: impeachment's structure, purpose, and history suggest a remedy broad enough to protect the body politic from federal officers whose lack of stability and competence might cause it serious harm.

"LOSS OF CAPACITY ... MIGHT BE FATAL TO THE REPUBLIC"

Not all the delegates to the Constitutional Convention believed that impeachment extended to cases of "incapacity." In a June 1 debate over the length of the chief magistrate's term, Delaware's Gunning Bedford declared himself "strongly opposed to so long a term as seven years." What if the country should discover that the president "did not possess the qualifications ascribed to him, or should lose them after his appointment"? Impeachment "would be no cure for this evil," Bedford worried, because it "would reach misfeasance only, not incapacity."[170]

Seven weeks later, however, during the Convention's most extensive debate on presidential impeachments, two delegates specifically mentioned "incapacity" as a justification for removal. As Madison saw it, "the limitation of the period of [the president's] service was not a sufficient security" against the prospect of an unfit chief magistrate: among other things, the president "might lose his capacity after his appointment."[171]

Where modern legal scholars such as Amar and Sunstein worry about the disruption entailed in presidential removal, Madison was more concerned about the destabilizing effects of keeping an unfit president in office. The fact that there is only one president made incapacity or corruption far more dangerous in the executive branch than in Congress or the judiciary. "It could not be presumed that all or even a majority of the members of [Congress] would either lose their capacity for discharging, or be bribed to betray, their trust," Madison argued, but "the Executive magistracy . . . was to be administered by a single man," and "loss of capacity" in that case "might be fatal to the Republic."[172]

The second delegate to endorse impeachment for incapacity was Gouverneur Morris. Morris had earlier pronounced himself opposed to presidential impeachments for any cause, but by the close of the July 20 debate, he acknowledged that he was now "sensible of the necessity of impeachments," which should be available in cases of "treachery," "corrupting his electors," and "incapacity." "For the latter," Morris said, the president "should be punished not as a man, but as an officer and punished only by degradation from his office."[173]

The broader view endorsed by Morris and Madison prevailed: "incapacity" has featured in a number of American impeachments, beginning with one of the earliest. Recall that Pickering's case, the first impeachment conviction in the young Republic, resulted in the removal of a judge incapable of doing his job for reasons of drunkenness and insanity. "Out of the confusion over the liability of Pickering's conduct," Hoffer and Hull write, "whether a person incapable of crime (and incompetent to stand trial) could be impeached, tried, and removed—came the clear rule that incompetence was an impeachable offense."[174] Later judicial impeachments, such as those of judges Mark Delahay (1873) and George W. English (1926), also involved impeachment for erratic behavior that called into question their fitness for office.[175]

THE "TWENTY-FIFTH AMENDMENT SOLUTION"?

Of course, no *president* has ever been impeached on the grounds that he was intellectually or temperamentally incapable of doing the job. Perhaps for that reason, some of President Trump's opponents have lately seized on another constitutional mechanism: using the Twenty-fifth Amendment to declare him mentally unfit for office.

Drafted in the wake of the Kennedy assassination and ratified in February 1967, the Twenty-fifth Amendment provides two methods by which the vice president can take over when the president is "unable to discharge the powers and duties of his office." Under Section 3, the president can make the decision himself, stepping aside temporarily, as presidents have several times in recent decades while undergoing anesthesia for surgical procedures.[176]

Under Section 4, however, the president can be removed involuntarily when he's deemed incapable of fulfilling his responsibilities. The vice president and a majority of cabinet heads or "such other body as Congress may by law provide" make the initial disability determination, transferring power temporarily to the vice president. If the president challenges that determination, the question goes to Congress, and if two-thirds of both houses ratify the switch, the vice president continues to serve as "Acting President." The full text of Section 4 follows:

Section 4. Whenever the Vice President and a majority of either the principal officers of the executive departments or of such other body as Congress may by law provide, transmit to the President pro tempore of the Senate and the Speaker of the House of Representatives their written declaration that the President is unable to discharge the powers and duties of his office, the Vice President shall immediately assume the powers and duties of the office as Acting President.

Thereafter, when the President transmits to the President pro tempore of the Senate and the Speaker of the House of Representatives his written declaration that no inability exists, he shall resume the powers and duties of his office unless the Vice President and a majority of either the principal officers of the executive department or of such other body as Congress may by law provide, transmit within four days to the President pro tempore of the Senate and the Speaker of the House of Representatives their written declaration that the President is unable to discharge the powers and duties of his office. Thereupon Congress shall decide the issue, assembling within forty-eight hours for that purpose if not in session. If the Congress, within twenty-one days after receipt of the latter written declaration, or, if Congress is not in session, within twenty-one days after Congress is required to assemble, determines by two-thirds vote of both Houses that the President is unable to discharge the powers and duties of his office, the Vice President shall continue to discharge the same as Acting President; otherwise, the President shall resume the powers and duties of his office.[177]

That provision has featured in a great many political thrillers—including several plot lines for TV's *24*—but it has, to date, never been deployed in real life.

In 2017, however, growing numbers of public intellectuals and elected officials began to see Section 4 as the best available method to repeal and replace the Trump presidency. Harvard's Laurence Tribe, in the Clinton years a leading alarmist about the dangers of presidential removal, raised the issue just after Trump's inauguration, identifying the provision as one possible "path to ridding civilization of the Trump menace."[178] In a much-discussed column in May 2017, the *New York Times*'s Ross Douthat offered "The 25th Amendment Solution for Removing Trump." "Leaving a man this witless and unmastered in an office with these powers and responsibilities is an act of gross negligence," Douthat charged, and argued that removal under the Twenty-fifth Amendment was a more appropriate constitutional mechanism than impeachment.[179]

The Twenty-fifth Amendment solution has gathered some momentum on Capitol Hill as well. In August 2017, citing "an alarming pattern of behavior and speech," Rep. Zoe Lofgren (D-CA) introduced a resolution calling for Trump's examination by "psychiatric professionals."[180] Reps. Earl Blumenauer (D-OR) and Jamie Raskin (D-MD) have each crafted bills setting up independent disability commissions to rule on the president's fitness.[181] At this writing, Raskin's Oversight Commission on Presidential Capacity Act has 65 cosponsors, including 12 of the 17 Democratic members of the House Judiciary Committee.[182]

Lofgren's resolution urges Vice President Mike Pence and the cabinet to take "immediate action" under Section 4. Raskin's bill, like Blumenauer's, relies on Congress's Section 4 power to appoint another body to help the vice president make the disability determination. But, as we'll see, in either form, the Twenty-fifth Amendment solution is both wildly impractical and constitutionally illegitimate.

ALL THE PRESIDENTS' ANALYSTS

Let's start with Raskin's Oversight Commission bill, currently the most popular in the House. Here's how it's supposed to work: Congress sets up a team of four psychiatrists, four physicians, two retired statespersons—such as former presidents and vice presidents—and a team-elected chair. When Congress summons them into action, their mission is to examine the president, determine whether he "lacks sufficient understanding or capacity to execute the powers and duties of the office," and report back within 72 hours.[183]

That's the plan: an 11-strong strike force of assorted shrinks and medics—plus, say, Bill Clinton and Dan Quayle—is supposed to descend on Donald Trump, take his vitals, and put him on the couch to suss out whether he's sane enough to be president.

Of course that examination will never happen, as the bill itself all but concedes: "any refusal by the President to undergo such examination shall be taken into consideration" in the Commission's disability ruling.[184] The implication seems to be that refusal should count against the president, although, if anything, *agreeing* to this arrangement should qualify as evidence of mental impairment. If, as seems overwhelmingly likely, Trump were to refuse, the psychiatrists on the team would be barred by professional ethics rules from diagnosing a patient they haven't personally examined.[185] Even if it passed, it's hard to see how this version of the Twenty-fifth Amendment solution would get off the ground.

COURTING CONSTITUTIONAL CRISIS

Moreover, whether the incapacity ruling is made by a majority of the cabinet or a professional disability commission, all versions of the Twenty-fifth Amendment solution depend on the vice president's cooperation to set the scheme in motion. Mike Pence, who's thus far stood by his man like a classic political "good wife," seems an unlikely conspirator. Even if Pence were willing, and could secure the necessary cooperation, there's an additional problem: ambiguities in Section 4's language could lead to a period of destabilizing uncertainty about who is actually in power when the disability ruling is challenged.

As Sen. Eugene McCarthy (D-MN) warned in 1965, the amendment might create a situation of "having two Presidents, each of whom desires to perform the duties of office, and . . . two cabinets," jockeying for recognition as the "real" government.[186] The term "constitutional crisis" gets thrown around far too loosely, but the Twenty-fifth Amendment solution might just deliver the genuine article.

In his 2012 book *Constitutional Cliffhangers,* law professor Brian Kalt identifies Section 4 as a "constitutional weak spot" that could crack if put to the test.[187] To illustrate the danger, here's an updated version of the scenario Kalt sketches: imagine Vice President Pence is privately more Machiavellian than he lets on; he and his colleagues decide to pull the trigger, activating Section 4 with a declaration to Congress. Trump, enraged, sends a counterdeclaration contesting the charge, summons the cabinet, and unleashes his signature line from the *Apprentice*: "You're fired!"

Trump then replaces his rebellious "team of rivals" with reliable subordinates. Pence and the original cabinet counter with a second declaration to Congress, reaffirming Trump's impairment. When Trump orders the Secret Service to frogmarch the "fake Cabinet" out of the building, how do they respond? Who's in charge here?

Section 4's language is less than lucid on this point. It specifies that, upon sending the initial declaration, "the Vice President shall immediately assume the powers and duties of the office as Acting President," but "when the President transmits . . . his written declaration that no inability exists, he shall resume the powers and duties of his office *unless*," [emphasis added] within four days, the VP and a majority of the cabinet reaffirm that the president is incapacitated.[188]

Whether Trump had the right to sack his cabinet turns on whether it was "his" when he gave the order. Under Section 4, does Pence hold the reins during that four-day period, or does the president get his powers back as soon as he informs Congress he's up to the job? Will Congress determine which is the "fake Cabinet," or will that question be settled by the Supreme Court, in a case that would make *Bush v. Gore* seem low-stakes by comparison?

"It is indisputable," Kalt writes, "that Section 4's creators intended for the vice president to remain in charge during this waiting period." But since the text is murky on this point, "if push ever comes to shove, things could go very badly."[189]

Things would have to be very bad to begin with for Pence and company to make their move; vice presidents are reluctant to look power-hungry, so, as Kalt notes, "Section 4 would probably only get invoked if the country was in the midst of an external crisis"—perhaps a major terrorist attack or the outbreak of war on the Korean Peninsula.[190] Whether or not these are desperate times, presidential removal via the Twenty-fifth Amendment is a desperate measure—one that should only appeal to those who think politics hasn't been quite entertaining *enough* lately.

ILLEGITIMATE "SOLUTION"

Finally, even if we ignore the practical difficulties and potential dangers of the Twenty-fifth Amendment solution, there's still another problem: it's constitutionally illegitimate. As even some of its advocates recognize, a good-faith reading of Section 4 won't permit its transformation into a substitute for impeachment.

In his argument for invoking the Twenty-fifth Amendment, the University of Chicago's Eric Posner writes that, under prevailing views of the Constitution's two presidential removal mechanisms, "there is no obvious solution for a president who has not committed a crime or been disabled by illness, but has lost the confidence of the public because of a failure of temperament, ideology or ability." Therefore, Posner argues, "the current understanding of the 25th Amendment should be enlarged so as to provide authority to address this problem."[191]

Give Posner points for honesty: there is, as he concedes, no way to get to that outcome without stretching the amendment's meaning. The Twenty-fifth Amendment wasn't designed for ejecting merely erratic or untrustworthy presidents. It aimed at situations of total, or near-total, disability, whether temporary or permanent.

It was the Kennedy assassination, after all, that motivated Congress to fill the gaps in presidential and vice-presidential succession. JFK's death highlighted the lack of any constitutional means for filling a vacancy in the vice-presidential office between elections, and it focused attention on the potential problem of presidential incapacity. In his story filed for the *New York Times* the day of the assassination, James Reston wrote, "for an all too brief hour today, it was not clear again what would have happened if the young President, instead of being mortally wounded, had lingered for a long time between life and death, strong enough to survive but too weak to govern."[192]

That was the kind of scenario Section 4 was designed for: the week before Congress passed the amendment, an important exchange between Sen. Birch Bayh (D-IN) and Sen. Robert Kennedy (D-NY) made that clear:

> **Bayh:** . . . It is conceivable that a
> President might be able to walk, for
> example . . . but at the same time, he

might not possess the mental capacity to make a decision and perform the powers and duties of his office. We are talking about inability to perform the constitutional duties of the office of President.

Kennedy: And that has to be total disability to perform the powers and duties of the office.

Bayh: The Senator is correct. We are not getting into a position, through the pending measure, in which when a President makes an unpopular decision, he would immediately be rendered unable to perform the duties of the office.[193]

In fact, as Bayh later explained, the double supermajority requirement—two-thirds of each house must vote to ratify the switch—was designed to preclude such a scenario: "We were concerned about the politics of the palace coup" and therefore deliberately made it harder to remove a president via Section 4 than it is to impeach him.[194]

Fordham University law professor John Feerick, a member of the American Bar Association task force that helped draft the amendment, summarizes the congressional debates: "It was made clear that unpopularity, incompetence, impeachable conduct, poor judgment, and laziness do not constitute an 'inability' within the meaning of the Amendment."[195] That understanding was widely shared in Congress and widely publicized prior to the amendment's ratification.

The wording of Section 4 leaves too much ambiguity for comfort when it comes to disputes during the four-day waiting period, but the key phrase on incapacity is clear enough. In context, "unable to discharge the powers and duties of his office" has to mean something more than "turned out to be dangerously bad at the job." What worries Posner, Raskin, Douthat, and their fellow travelers isn't that Trump is unable to discharge the powers of his office— it's that he's reckless and immature enough to do enormous damage when he does. Impeachment is the proper constitutional remedy for that sort of presidential incapacity.

5

Negligence and Mismanagement

Convinced that impeachment is reserved for willful misconduct, supporters of the Twenty-fifth Amendment solution have strained to categorize President Trump's deficiencies as evidence of mental illness. But most of what troubles them about Trump might be better understood in terms of Madison's second category, "negligence."

Douthat charges that our 45th president lacks "a reasonable level of intellectual curiosity, a certain seriousness of purpose, a basic level of managerial competence, a decent attention span, a functional moral compass, [and] a measure of restraint and self-control."[196] Nothing on that list obviously indicates a clinical condition; instead, what Douthat describes is a standard of care to which a reasonably competent and attentive president would adhere. A president incapable of living up to that standard, or who can't be bothered to try, is practically certain to botch the job and damage the country in the process.

MADISON AND "MALADMINISTRATION"

Still, is it constitutionally permissible to impeach a president for chronic negligence and gross mismanagement? Here again, the conventional wisdom says no, and some of the drafting history of Article II, Section 4, supports that view. Recall that, according to Madison's notes, when George Mason moved to add "or maladministration" to the list of impeachable offenses, Madison objected that "so vague a term will be equivalent to a tenure during pleasure of the Senate." Mason then substituted "high Crimes and Misdemeanors"; the Convention approved that change by a vote of eight to three; and that's the language we have to work with today.

During the Clinton imbroglio, the president's defenders made much of the Mason-Madison exchange. Madison's objection to the phrase, Laurence Tribe argued, showed that he "recognized that the power to remove a president for something as nebulous as maladministration could lead to something . . . awfully close to Roger Sherman's idea that you could remove a president at will."[197]

But that snippet of legislative history isn't the last word on impeachment's availability in cases of gross mismanagement. First, on its own terms, as Charles Black observed, the exchange doesn't preclude the possibility that an act could be "an instance *both* of 'maladministration' *and* of 'high crime' or 'misdemeanor.' It does mean that not *all* acts of 'maladministration' are covered by the phrase actually accepted."[198]

Madison himself understood "high Crimes and Misdemeanors" to extend to some forms of maladministration. Both during and after the drafting of the Constitution, he took a view of the impeachment power broad enough to cover gross mismanagement, incompetence, and other "conduct simply incompatible with the status of the chief executive."[199]

Indeed, although Tribe and others read the Madison-Mason exchange as significantly narrowing the scope of impeachable offenses, Madison initially feared that "high Crimes and Misdemeanors" was *still* too close to employment-at-will. Shortly after the delegates approved that text, Madison objected to the Senate as the tribunal for trying the president, "especially as he was to be impeached by the other branch of the Legislature, and for *any act which might be called a misdemeanor*. The president under these circumstances was made improperly dependent" [emphasis added].[200]

Moreover, the Convention debates were secret; Madison's notes weren't published until half a century later and were never intended as the authoritative guide to constitutional meaning. What the delegates to the ratifying conventions had before them was the text itself, and that text was understood from British practice to incorporate maladministration.[201] By the time of the ratification debates, the phrase "high crimes and misdemeanors" had been in use for centuries in British impeachments, and as the Nixon Inquiry Report noted, it was understood to cover negligent discharge of duties, "procuring offices for persons unfit and unworthy of them," and other transgressions falling short of grave criminality.[202] In its entry on "high misdemeanors," Blackstone's *Commentaries on the Laws of England* (1765)—per Madison, "a book which is in every man's hand"—notes that first among such offenses was "maladministration of such high offices as are in public trust and employment."[203] Early American commentators, such as Justice Story, understood high crimes and misdemeanors to include offenses "growing out of personal misconduct, or gross neglect, or usurpation, or habitual disregard of the public interests, in the discharge of the duties of political office."[204]

At the time of its adoption and ratification, then, the constitutional text was understood to cover *some* cases of gross mismanagement and dereliction of duty. Indeed, if the lodestar of impeachment is, as Madison put it, "defending the community," some such cases would have to be within the remedy's ambit. Professor Black had a gift for the clarifying "law school hypothetical," and one of his oft-cited examples speaks to this point:

> Suppose a president were to move to
> Saudi Arabia, so he could have four
> wives, and were to propose to conduct
> the office of the presidency by mail
> and wireless from there. This would
> not be a crime, provided his passport

were in order. Is it possible that such gross and wanton neglect of duty could not be grounds for impeachment and removal?[205]

"THE WANTON REMOVAL OF MERITORIOUS OFFICERS"

At some level, neglect of duty becomes as serious and threatening a breach of public trust as deliberate abuse.[206] What about neglect and maladministration short of total abandonment of office? Can a president lawfully be impeached for misusing the discretion entrusted to him in the management of the executive branch? A key debate during the first Congress suggests that he can.

Three weeks after George Washington's inauguration, Congress deliberated on the structure of three new executive departments to assist our first president in the performance of his duties. The second clause of Article II, Section 2, stipulated that officers of the United States were to be appointed "by and with the Advice and Consent of the Senate," but it was silent as to the president's powers to remove them. Should he be able to fire department heads at will, or only by the same means through which they were appointed?

Madison, now serving Virginia in the House of Representatives, moved that the secretary of the Department of Foreign Affairs should be removable by the president without Senate approval. The discretion to remove officers was, he said, inherent in the executive power vested by Article II, Section 1. Moreover, that discretion was essential to effective management of the executive branch: without it, Madison declared, "I do not see how the president can take care that the laws be faithfully executed."[207]

To those who objected that removal at will left too much power in the president's hands, Madison replied that impeachment provided an essential check on abuse of discretion whether the president removed good officers or retained bad ones. "If an unworthy man be continued in office by an unworthy president, the house of representatives can at any time impeach [that officer], and the senate can remove him." And should the president "displace from office a man whose merits require that he should be continued in it . . . he will be impeachable by this house, before the senate, for such an act of mal-administration. . . . The wanton removal of meritorious officers would," he affirmed, subject the president "to impeachment and removal from his own high trust."[208]

Madison's arguments helped carry the day: the legislation, as passed, allowed the president to remove the Secretary at will.[209] Eight decades later, the case against President Andrew Johnson would involve the "wanton removal of a meritorious officer." In that light, perhaps the central charges against Johnson weren't as constitutionally frivolous as they've come to be understood. By firing

Secretary of War Edwin Stanton, a figure central to the military enforcement of Reconstruction, Johnson's opponents charged that he'd committed an impeachable offense. But they muddied the waters unnecessarily by hanging so much of their case on violations of the constitutionally dubious Tenure of Office Act. If the abuse of discretion is serious enough, it can be grounds for impeachment regardless of whether any statute has been violated.

FAILURE TO LAUNCH

What if, instead of removing good officers and appointing bad ones, the president simply neglects to appoint enough people—good *or* bad—to run an effective administration? That's one of the accusations lodged against President Trump, and some scholars have suggested it constitutes an impeachable offense. In an article for *Slate* published in May 2017, Philip Carter, Georgetown law professor and senior fellow at the Center for a New American Security, offered seven possible "Articles of Impeachment for Donald J. Trump"—four more than even Richard Nixon got. Among Carter's bill of particulars: "Article 7: Dereliction of his constitutional duty to faithfully execute the office of president by failing to timely appoint officers of the United States to administer the nation's federal agencies."[210] Since the Constitution's Appointments Clause is phrased as a command—he "*shall* appoint Ambassadors . . . and all other Officers of the United States"—a president arguably violates a constitutional obligation when he fails to adequately staff his administration.²¹¹ As Carter sees it, Trump's failure was willful: part of then chief strategist Steve Bannon's supposed plan for the "deconstruction of the administrative state."²¹²

There's no doubt the Trump administration has moved far less quickly than its predecessors in staffing the government. By one count, six months into his tenure, Trump had nominated only 277 people for the more than 1,100 Senate-confirmed positions the president has to fill. The numbers for his two immediate predecessors, Barack Obama and George W. Bush, were 433 and 414, respectively—and each had more appointees confirmed at the six-month mark than Trump had even nominated.²¹³

Trump has periodically blamed Senate Democrats "for taking forever to approve my people," but it's hard to see how minority-party obstructionism could block him from identifying candidates and putting their names forward in the first place.²¹⁴ He's also offered a contradictory explanation consistent with Carter's suspicions: that the staffing gap is part of his plan for leaner government. "When I see a story about 'Donald Trump didn't fill hundreds and hundreds of jobs,'" the president said in February 2017, "it's because, in many cases, we don't want to fill those jobs."²¹⁵

But if that's supposed to lead to the "deconstruction of the administrative state," it's not a great plan. It amounts to the fond hope that the administrative state will spontaneously self-deconstruct and the swamp will drain itself. A president cannot hope to exert control over the federal bureaucracy—let alone dismantle large parts of it—without putting political appointees in place who will drive his agenda. Leaving the levers of control in the hands of career civil servants would all but guarantee business as usual for the permanent bureaucracy.

By the end of his first year in office, President Trump was taking credit for "the most far-reaching regulatory reform" in American history.[216] There was a good deal of the usual bluster and resume-padding behind that claim.[217] But what success the administration enjoyed in slowing the growth of new regulations and rolling back existing ones owed more to key appointments he'd made than to posts he'd left unfilled.[218]

As for the overall staffing gap, neither story Trump tells adequately explains it. It's more likely that the slow pace of appointments stems from a combination of factors: lack of prior preparation because the Trump team didn't really expect to win; little governing experience on the part of Trump and his close advisers; "loyalty tests" that disqualify anyone who's publicly criticized the president; and the fact that Trump isn't a particularly good manager to begin with.[219] Instead of pushing for impeachment on grounds of maladministration, perhaps Carter, and others who oppose the deregulatory agenda Trump campaigned on, should be grateful the president is far from the uber-capable executive he claims to be.

IMPEACHMENT FOR NEGLIGENT SUPERVISION?

By itself, simply being a subpar manager shouldn't constitute an impeachable offense. Here, Charles Black's observation has some force: "Whatever its vagueness at the edges," he wrote in *Impeachment: A Handbook*, the constitutional language "seems absolutely to forbid the removal of a president on the grounds that Congress does not, on the whole, think his administration of public affairs is good."[220]

Indeed, if presidents could be impeached for mere mismanagement, practically all of them would be vulnerable. Some degree of mismanagement is all but inevitable given the massive growth of the executive branch since the early 20th century. As former Obama adviser David Axelrod commented in 2013: "Part of being president is there's so much underneath you because the government is so vast. You go through these [controversies] all because of this stuff that is impossible to know if you're the president or working in the White House, and yet you're responsible for it and it's a difficult situation."[221]

Axelrod's observation, offered in the midst of several scandals then roiling the Obama administration, struck many on the right as a laughably convenient excuse.[222] Even so, he had a point: "the sheer size of federal government creates an impossible management paradox," Cornell law professor Cynthia Farina has observed. With 15 Cabinet departments, more than 160 different federal regulatory agencies, and more than two million civilian employees in the executive branch, the idea that strong presidential leadership can bring "coherence, rationality, and accountability to the vast U.S. regulatory enterprise is unrealistic, if not completely implausible."[223]

Trump's immediate predecessors found that out the hard way. George W. Bush's biggest (domestic) mismanagement scandal came in the aftermath of Hurricane Katrina in 2005; "Obama's Katrina" was the BP oil spill in the Gulf of Mexico five years later. In each case, critics charged, with some justice, that the disasters could have been mitigated or even avoided entirely with better management.[224]

Obama faced no serious calls for his impeachment over the BP affair.[225] In Bush's case, "failure to plan for the predicted disaster of Hurricane Katrina" was the basis for one of 35 articles of impeachment introduced by Reps. Dennis Kucinich (D-OH) and Robert Wexler (D-FL) in 2008. But the idea wasn't taken very seriously, and the effort died without a vote by the House Judiciary Committee.[226]

That's probably as it should be. As Black observed, holding the president personally liable for every failing of his subordinates would set an impossible standard: "No chief of any considerable enterprise could pass such a test."[227]

What we have in the way of presidential precedent suggests something closer to criminal negligence or recklessness: impeachment may be warranted where the president should have been aware of, or consciously disregards, a substantial and unjustifiable risk.[228] The second article of impeachment against Richard Nixon charged him, in part, with "failing to act when he knew *or had reason to know* that his close subordinates" were engaged in obstruction of justice [emphasis added]. Evidence of a deliberate plot to injure the public or subvert its trust isn't strictly necessary. As Black put it, "When carelessness is so gross and habitual as to be evidence of *indifference* to wrongdoing, it may be in effect equivalent to ratification of wrongdoing."[229]

"MANAGING UP"

What if the problem isn't the president's supervision of his subordinates, but their ability to manage—and even "contain"—*him*? That's the situation described by a number of highly placed Republicans, including the chairman of the Senate Foreign Relations Committee.

In October 2017, after President Trump blasted him in a series of tweets, Sen. Bob Corker (R-TN) shot back: "It's a shame the White House has become an adult day care center. Someone obviously missed their shift this morning."[230] Corker elaborated in an interview: "I know for a fact that every single day at the White House, it's a situation of trying to contain him." Corker's colleagues know it too, he said: the "vast majority" of the GOP caucus understands "the volatility that we're dealing with." Trump's recklessness and lack of emotional discipline could, the senator warned, put us "on the path to World War III."[231]

Senator Corker is hardly alone in that assessment; he's unusual mainly in his willingness to go on the record. Tufts University professor Daniel Drezner has assembled a massive list of news stories in which Trump's own aides or political allies talk about the president as if he's a "toddler."[232] For obvious reasons, most of these accounts rely on anonymous sourcing: if we could identify the persons making the claims, the president could identify them as well. But that also leaves the reader unclear, in many cases, which stories are well-grounded and which were driven mainly by the White House rumor mill and staffers' personal agendas.

Still, even when taken with the necessary grain of salt, the accumulated testimonials strongly support Corker's portrayal. They describe a White House staff working desperately to rein in a president liable to upend settled administration policy or cause an international incident with a tweet simply because he's spun up about the latest outrage touted on the *Fox & Friends* morning show.

But constitutionally credible articles of impeachment cannot consist of on-background quotes from anonymous staffers: "Whereas then-Secretary of State Rex Tillerson has not denied the *NBC News* report that he referred to the president as 'a [expletive deleted] moron' at a Pentagon meeting on July 20, 2017. . . . "[233] Impeachment extends to cases of gross negligence, but the constitutional language, "high Crimes and Misdemeanors," requires reference to specific acts or omissions that violate the public trust.

Several scholars have pointed to one such act as potential grounds. In May 2017 the *Washington Post* reported that Trump may have "jeopardized a critical source of intelligence on the Islamic State" while bragging to Russian diplomats about his "great intel." During an Oval Office meeting with Russian Foreign Minister Sergei Lavrov and Ambassador Sergey Kislyak, President Trump reportedly shared top-secret intelligence about an Islamic State plot to bring down airplanes with explosives hidden in laptop computers. In so doing, the president may have let slip enough detail to reveal the sources and methods behind the intel, betraying the trust of the country that shared it with us and complicating intelligence-sharing for counterterrorism going forward.[234]

The possibility that this happened "is itself sufficient to justify a congressional impeachment inquiry," Keith Whittington suggests:

> If the president, through wanton
> carelessness or severe misjudgment,
> undermined national security . . . by
> mishandling the nation's most sensitive
> intelligence, then he abused his office in
> a manner that the Constitution empow-
> ered Congress to remedy through
> impeachment. Congress cannot undo
> the damage the president has already
> done, but the impeachment power
> is designed to address a situation in
> which an officeholder has demonstrated
> through his past actions that he can no
> longer act in the public trust.[235]

6

Perfidy and Presidential Power

With "perfidy," the third of Madison's categories, we move closer to impeachment's heart: willful corruption and abuse of power. At the Convention, Madison offered several examples of transgressions falling under that heading: the president might "pervert his administration into a scheme of peculation or oppression" or "betray his trust to foreign powers."[236]

But even in cases where it's clear that the president's intentions were corrupt, difficult questions remain. Must an impeachable offense involve an abuse of presidential powers, or can it involve private transgressions? Can offenses committed before the president assumed office ever serve as grounds for removal? Is it constitutionally permissible to impeach a president for conduct unbecoming the presidency? In what circumstances is impeachment available to rectify corrupt financial dealings, obstruction of justice, or the president's misuse of powers, such as the authority to pardon, that the Constitution clearly grants him? And in cases where Congress, through a long pattern of ceding power to the executive branch, has been complicit in presidential abuses, has it also ceded the authority to impeach and remove the president for those abuses? In this section, we'll treat each of those questions in turn.

IS "PRIVATE" CONDUCT IMPEACHABLE?

On August 17, 1998, shortly after testifying to a federal grand jury about his "inappropriate" relationship with Monica Lewinsky, President Bill Clinton gave a nationally televised address in which he defiantly declared: "It's nobody's business but ours. Even presidents have private lives."[237]

Does impeachment extend to misdeeds committed in a president's private life? That became a key question in the ensuing debate over Clinton's impeachment. Republicans objected to that framing: perjury and obstruction of justice were public acts, they maintained. But since those offenses were committed in the course of covering up a private affair, the president's defenders insisted they did not rise to the level of high crimes and misdemeanors.

Much of the legal academy's top talent leapt to Clinton's defense, insisting that impeachable offenses were limited to abuses of office and did not extend to private scandals or crimes.[238] More than 430 law professors signed a letter to the House Judiciary Committee insisting that the constitutional standard was "grossly heinous criminality or grossly derelict misuse of official power."[239] Perjury and obstruction to cover up an illicit affair weren't nearly grave enough.

As two of Clinton's most prominent academic defenders saw it, even *murder* wasn't a clear-cut case, as long as the president does the deed himself, for personal reasons. The impeachment remedy was *so* narrow, Cass Sunstein insisted, that if the president were to "murder someone simply because he does not like him," it would make for a "hard case."[240] In his congressional testimony, Laurence Tribe emphasized the fact that "when Vice President Aaron Burr killed Alexander Hamilton in a duel in July 1804," instead of getting impeached, "Burr served out his term, which ended in early 1805." Today, "there may well be room to argue," Tribe grudgingly conceded, that a murdering president could be removed without grave damage to the Constitution—but that exception "must not be permitted to swallow [the] rule."[241]

The signatories to the law professors' letter left themselves a similar "out": "we do not say that a 'private' crime could never be so heinous as to warrant impeachment. . . . Certain crimes such as murder [could] warrant removal of a President."[242] Another statement on behalf of Clinton—signed by 400 historians, including Arthur Schlesinger, Jr., Doris Kearns Goodwin, and Sean Wilentz—refused to make any exception: the self-styled "Historians in Defense of the Constitution" maintained that "the Framers *explicitly* reserved [impeachment] for high crimes and misdemeanors in the exercise of executive power" [emphasis added].[243]

It's no secret that academia is overwhelmingly liberal; in this case, the president's academic defenders seem to have succumbed to the temptation Professor Black cautioned against: resolving constitutional questions "in favor

of the immediate political result that is [most] palatable."[244]
As it happens, the Framers did not, explicitly or otherwise,
limit impeachable offenses to abuses of official power.
The historical record is quite clear: federal officers can be
impeached for misconduct that doesn't involve the powers
of their office when that misconduct raises serious questions about their fitness for public trust.

The first impeachment case under the federal
Constitution involved offenses committed "off the clock,"
as it were. Senator William Blount's scheme for a freeboo-
ting expedition against Spanish territory didn't involve the
abuse of any powers he held by virtue of being a senator.
Yet that was no barrier to his impeachment. As one of
the House managers noted, "There is not a syllable in the
Constitution which confines impeachment to official acts,
and . . . it is against the plain dictates of common sense,
that such restraint should be imposed on it."[245]

A number of the judicial impeachment cases, including those of judges Robert W. Archbald (1912–1913)
and Halsted Ritter (1936), underscore that point.[246] In
Archbald's case, the House Judiciary Committee emphati-
cally rejected the argument that only misuse of office could
be grounds for removal: "any conduct on the part of a judge
which reflects on his integrity as a man or his fitness to perform the judicial functions should be sufficient to sustain
his impeachment. It would be both absurd and monstrous
to hold that an impeachable offense must needs be committed in an official capacity."[247]

For an official in a position of great public trust, it's not possible to compartmentalize behavior so neatly into public and private. Indeed, by making an exception for murder and other "heinous offenses," the signatories to the law professors' letter give away the game by conceding that at least *some* private wrongs can be serious enough to merit impeachment.

As Judge Posner observes in his book on the Clinton impeachment, *An Affair of State*, "at some point, the personal becomes the political."[248] Taking a cue from Professor Black, Posner sets out a series of hypotheticals where no abuse of distinctly presidential powers occurs: the president perjures himself in his best friend's trial on child molestation charges; the president fakes a DNA test to escape responsibility in a paternity suit; the president strangles a former lover with his bare hands to prevent her from testifying before a grand jury. In such cases, Posner writes, he "would have to be impeached and convicted if he refused to resign. Americans will not be ruled by a Nero or a Caligula, however executively competent."[249]

Neither do Americans demand to be governed by moral exemplars, however. Impeachment is an extraordinary remedy, not a means for ejecting chief executives with regular, all-too-human failings. The question, as Black put it, is whether a given offense, private or public, "would so stain a president as to make his continuance in office dangerous to public order."[250]

PREPRESIDENTIAL PERFIDY

If a president can lawfully be impeached for nonofficial conduct, does it matter when that conduct occurred? Can transgressions he committed years before assuming the presidency qualify as high crimes and misdemeanors?

The academics fastest out of the gate with calls for Trump's impeachment insisted that prepresidential conduct counts. But then, they'd have to say that: if you publish *The Case for Impeachment* three months into the Trump presidency, as American University's Allan J. Lichtman did, you're going to have to rely heavily on what the man did *before* he was elected. In that rushed-to-publication tome, Lichtman suggests that Trump could rightfully be impeached for, inter alia, past violations of "the Fair Housing Act, New York charity law, tax laws, the Cuban embargo, casino regulations, the RICO statute, and laws against employing illegal immigrants."[251] Faster still was University of Utah law professor Christopher L. Peterson, who published his case for Trump's impeachment nearly two months before the election.[252] If elected, Peterson wrote, Trump could lawfully be impeached for fraud and racketeering in connection with the Trump University real-estate training program the candidate ran from 2005 to 2010.[253]

Lichtman and Peterson may have overreached with their specific charges, but that doesn't make them wrong about the general principle. If private misconduct can "so stain a president" as to demonstrate his unfitness for public trust, so too can past wrongdoing. Murder makes for a good test case here as well: suppose, instead of violating the Fair Housing Act or employing illegal immigrants, we were to discover that years ago, Donald Trump had disposed of a commercial rival by ordering a contract killing? In that case, impeachment would clearly be constitutionally legitimate. As Michael Gerhardt has argued, "the timing of the murder is of less concern than the fact of it; this is the kind of behavior that is completely incompatible with the public trust invested in officials who are sufficiently high-ranking to be subject to the impeachment process."[254]

Admittedly, American precedent, thin to begin with, is thinner still on the question of impeachment for prior misconduct. The first clear-cut case of removal on those grounds is also our most recent impeachment case, that of Judge G. Thomas Porteous in 2010.[255] The House accused Porteous of having "engaged in a longstanding pattern of corrupt conduct," including a corrupt relationship with a bail bondsman and kickbacks to cover gambling debts. The Senate convicted on all articles, including the second, which covered transgressions Porteous had committed as a state-court judge.[256]

In a *New York Review of Books* essay on impeachment, Noah Feldman and Jacob Weisberg dismiss the Porteous precedent as an outlier, arguing that it is "clear both historically and logically that impeachment was designed to deal with abuses committed while in office, not prior crimes."[257] If evidence emerged that a president attempted to steal the election, there would be a closer connection to abuse of office, Feldman and Weisberg suggest, but even that would be "a grey area." Actually, it's an easy call.

The case for removal on the basis of a federal officer's prior conduct is strongest when concealment of that conduct was instrumental to securing his or her post. Indeed, the danger of the electors "being corrupted by the Candidates . . . furnished a peculiar reason in favor of impeachments," George Mason argued at the Philadelphia Convention: "Shall the man who has practised corruption & by that means procured his appointment in the first instance, be suffered to escape punishment, by repeating his guilt?"[258] Procuring appointment through fraud was also one of the charges for which Porteous was removed in 2010: the fourth article of impeachment accused him of lying to the Senate and the FBI "in order to obtain the office of United States District Court Judge."[259]

We needn't conjure up a law-school hypothetical to test whether this principle applies to the president: an example from recent history will serve just as well. It has long been rumored that, as a presidential candidate in 1968, Richard Nixon worked behind the scenes to scuttle the Johnson administration's Vietnam peace talks. In 2016, a historian doing archival research at the Nixon Library discovered hard evidence of the plot in the form of handwritten notes taken by then campaign chief H. R. Haldeman. Memorializing a phone conversation with Nixon in late October 1968, Haldeman took down the candidate's orders to keep Anna Chennault—a GOP fund-raiser with connections to the South Vietnamese government—"working on SVN . . . Any other way to monkey wrench it? Anything RN can do."[260] President Johnson, who had Chennault under FBI surveillance, strongly suspected Nixon's involvement, but decided not to go public with the charge because he lacked "absolute proof."[261] But had this smoking gun come to light during Nixon's presidency, is there any good reason he couldn't have been impeached for it?

The case for impeachment on the basis of past misconduct is much weaker, however, when the official's faults were well known prior to assuming office. As Gerhardt observes, "if the impeachment process' aims to remove people to protect the public trust, that goal seems to have become moot when the public has passed on (or even ratified) the conduct involved."[262]

Most of the preinaugural conduct identified by Lichtman and Peterson seems to fall into the latter category. Trump's questionable business practices—and past sexual misbehavior—were well publicized during the 2016 campaign. But, as Bill Clinton discovered with the Paula Jones case, litigation can dredge up past behavior and make it newly relevant. Should Donald Trump end up getting deposed in one of the multiple lawsuits that followed him to the presidency, we may have a chance to watch conservatives and liberals switch sides on the question of whether perjury about sex is an impeachable offense.[263]

THE QUESTION OF EMOLUMENTS

Some of the earliest calls for President Trump's impeachment focused on the Foreign Emoluments Clause. Because of his financial entanglements with foreign governments, Trump "will be in violation of this clause of the Constitution from the moment he takes office," Norman L. Eisen and Richard W. Painter, chief White House ethics lawyers for Presidents Obama and Bush, respectively, warned after the election.[264] In a Brookings Institution White Paper published a month before inauguration, Eisen and Painter, joined by Harvard's Laurence Tribe, argued that unless Trump divests himself of "all ownership interests in the Trump business empire . . . Congress would be well within its rights to impeach him for engaging in 'high crimes and misdemeanors.'"[265]

The provision at issue, Article I, Section 9, clause 8, stipulates that

> no Person holding any Office of Profit
> or Trust under [the United States], shall,
> without the Consent of the Congress,
> accept of any present, Emolument,
> Office or Title, of any kind whatever,
> from any King, Prince, or foreign State.

What is an "emolument," and what, exactly, does the clause prohibit? Founding-era usage of the term ranged from a broad sense, encompassing profit or advantage, to a narrower office/public employment sense covering "monetizable benefits from holding office or working in the government's employ."[266]

Eisen, Painter, and Tribe argue for the broadest connotation: "the best reading of the Clause covers even ordinary, fair market value transactions that result in any economic profit or benefit to the federal officer." It forbids the president "from accepting *anything* of value from a foreign government."[267] Thus, they insist, "the [Foreign] Emoluments Clause will be violated whenever a foreign diplomat stays in a Trump hotel" and when "foreign-owned banks . . . pay rent for office space in Trump's buildings," even if those are arm's-length transactions in which the foreign parties pay no more than the going rate.[268]

But, applied consistently, that reading of the key term would lead to absurd results.[269] Consider: in the *Domestic* Emoluments Clause, the Constitution also bars the president, during his tenure, from receiving "any other Emolument from the United States, or any of them."[270] If an emolument indicates *anything* of value, a president would violate that clause—and risk impeachment—simply by owning, and receiving interest payments on, U.S. Treasury bonds.[271]

Moreover, construing emoluments broadly enough to cover fair-market-value transactions is inconsistent with important evidence of the clause's original meaning. The legal scholar Robert G. Natelson notes that "when the Constitution was ratified everyone knew that tobacco

growers were likely future candidates for the presidency—
among them Patrick Henry, Thomas Jefferson, and James
Madison." At the time, the law in several states, including
Virginia, required growers to deposit their product in
state warehouses in exchange for "tobacco notes" usable
as currency. If the Domestic Emoluments Clause had been
understood to cover arms-length transactions with the
states, then it would have required any "tobacco grower
elected president to sell or fallow his land before serving as
president." Yet when Thomas Jefferson and James Madison
assumed the presidency, "there was no outcry to the effect
that they were receiving unconstitutional emoluments
from tobacco notes."[272]

Further evidence against a sweeping definition of
emoluments can be found in a constitutional amendment proposed by Congress in 1810 that was nearly ratified. The "Original Thirteenth Amendment" would have
extended the prohibition on titles of nobility and foreign
emoluments to ordinary citizens. By 1812 it had secured
ratification in 12 states—two short of the three-quarters
required by Article V. Among other restrictions, the
amendment would have invalidated the citizenship of
any American who, "without the consent of Congress,
accept[s] and retain[s] any . . . emolument of any kind"
from a foreign power.[273] As Cato's Trevor Burrus puts it,
"it would be decidedly odd if this near-amendment to the
Constitution was understood to strip the citizenship from
a Philadelphia tobacconist who sold a pipe to a French

ambassador, or a New York businessman who made interest on foreign bonds."[274]

The better understanding of emolument, with regard to the constitutional provisions using that term, is the narrower one: "office-related compensation," or, as Professor Natelson describes it: "*All* compensation with financial value, received by reason of public office, including salary and fringe benefits. Proceeds from unrelated market transactions were outside the scope of this term."[275]

In theory, a breach of one of the constitutional prohibitions on emoluments could be impeachable. Egregious violations are akin to bribery, a specifically enumerated impeachable offense. At the Virginia Ratifying Convention, Edmund Randolph declared: "There is another provision against the danger . . . of the president receiving emoluments from foreign powers. If discovered, he may be impeached."[276]

Still, the emoluments-based articles of impeachment so far formally introduced in the House aren't terribly compelling. Those articles, two of the five put forward by Tennessee congressman Steve Cohen in November 2017, claim that the president has, without the consent of Congress, accepted emoluments from foreign states and the federal government, and therefore "warrants impeachment and trial, and removal from office."[277] Article II of Cohen's indictment rests on the Foreign Emoluments Clause; Article III, on violations of the Domestic Emoluments Clause. Unless one accepts Eisen et al.'s

extravagant gloss on emoluments, neither makes out a sufficient case for impeachment.

Among the violations listed in Cohen's Article II are
the following:

- "The Embassy of Kuwait canceled a 'save
  the date' reservation for an event at the Four
  Seasons Hotel in Washington, D.C., and held
  its National Day Celebration, instead, at Trump
  International Hotel."
- "At least two tenants of Trump Tower [in
  Manhattan] are entities owned by foreign
  states," the Industrial and Commercial Bank of
  China and the Abu Dhabi Tourism and Culture
  Authority (UAE).
- Georgia's ambassador to the U.S. used Twitter
  to praise the Trump International Hotel ("so far
  the best service I've seen in the United States!").
- Shortly after Trump won the 2016 election, "a
  long-stalled plan for a Trump-branded tower in a
  seaside Georgian resort town was back on track
  to move ahead."[278]

Cohen's Article III, "Violation of the Domestic
Emoluments Clause," contains similarly underwhelm-
ing allegations, such as "Donald J. Trump caused the
United States government to spend Federal funds at
Trump-branded properties . . . including a reported

$73,000 by the Secret Service on golf cart rentals, as well as $1,092 by the National Security Council for two nights of lodging at Mar-a-Lago."

Both articles complain that the president has "refused to release his tax returns, with the intent to conceal the exact nature of his holdings from Congress and the American people." By itself, that omission is weak grounds for an impeachable offense, but it does point to a problem: our lack of information about the precise scope and extent of the president's business interests. The available evidence suggests there's ample reason for concern about Trump's potential conflicts of interest.[279] But given Trump's resistance to transparency, the available evidence is incomplete.

A serious congressional effort to force disclosure is unlikely unless and until Congress changes hands. But if and when it does, a new majority may be able to force disclosure of the president's tax returns and other financial information. Since 1924, three congressional committees have had statutory authority to demand from the Secretary of the Treasury "any [tax] return or return information" concerning any taxpayer.[280] Congress also has tools available to it to seek financial details on Trump Organization operations not found on his personal tax returns.[281]

In order to decide whether the president's financial entanglements are of constitutional moment, Congress needs a better picture of their extent. That sort of inquiry should precede any impeachment effort.

IMPEACHMENT FOR "CONDUCT UNBECOMING"?

In June 2017, after President Trump unleashed a string of tweets insulting a cable news host—"low I.Q. Crazy Mika" Brzezinski, whom he claimed to have seen "bleeding badly from a facelift"—Sen. Ben Sasse (R-NE) responded with a tweet of his own: "Please just stop. This isn't normal and it's beneath the dignity of your office."[282]

Through all the chatter about emoluments and Russian plots, "not normal" is at the heart of concerns about the Trump presidency. That recurring lament often involves the president's Twitter feed, Trump's regular outlet for tantrums about bad restaurant reviews, Saturday Night Live skits, "so-called judges" who should be blamed for future terrorist attacks, and the United States' nuclear-armed rivals.[283]

In public appearances, Trump is equally incontinent. Whether he's addressing CIA officers in front of the Memorial Wall at Langley or a gaggle of Webelos at the National Boy Scout Jamboree in West Virginia, the president rants about "fake news," blasts his political enemies, and brags about the size of his Inaugural crowd. Fans of the president's speechifying praise him for "shaking things up" and "telling it like it is"—as if it's only hypocritical Beltway pieties he's skewering. Just as often, though, Trump tramples the sort of tacit norms that help distinguish the United States from a banana republic, such as: a president shouldn't tell active-duty military personnel to "call those senators" on behalf of his agenda, suggest that his political opponents should be put in jail, or make off-the-cuff threats of nuclear annihilation.[284]

But what are we supposed to do: *impeach* him for it? The very idea is "insane," Never-Trump conservative Ramesh Ponnuru writes at *National Review*.[285] "What would you put in the articles of impeachment?" asks *Bloomberg View* columnist Megan McArdle, "President Donald J. Trump said the wrong thing?"[286]

That's essentially what two House members have done. After President Trump's combative press conference in August 2017, blaming both sides for the violence at a neo-Nazi rally in Charlottesville, Representative Cohen, a member of the House Judiciary Committee, announced his plans to introduce an article of impeachment based on Trump's failed moral leadership.[287] In October, Representative Al Green read out four articles of impeachment on the House floor. They accused Trump of having undermined the integrity of his office and bringing disrepute on the presidency in a series of speeches and public statements. Green cited Trump's post-Charlottesville comments, along with his disparagement of protesting NFL players, his accusation that President Obama had his wires tapped, his claim that millions of people voted illegally, and various other comments said to inflame racial antipathy.[288]

Unsurprisingly, both proposals were greeted with skepticism. When Green tried to force consideration of his charges in December, only 58 Democrats wanted to bring them to a vote.[289] The idea of removing a president for

"conduct unbecoming"—low tweets and misdemeanors?—
takes us far afield from the sort of criminal abuse of power
that most people believe impeachment requires.

Even so, our constitutional history suggests that what is
"not normal" can sometimes be impeachable. On a number
of occasions, the House has deployed the "indispensable"
remedy against federal officers who, through their public
deportment, revealed defects of character and temperament "grossly incompatible with the proper function and
purpose of the office."[290]

As the Nixon Inquiry Report explained, the House has
the power to impeach, and the Senate to remove, a federal officer whose conduct "seriously undermine[s] public
confidence in his ability to perform his official functions."[291]
That's been clear since our earliest impeachment cases,
including that of Supreme Court Justice Samuel Chase
(1805), charged with "prostitut[ing] the high judicial character with which he was invested, to the low purpose of an
electioneering partisan"[292]; and Judge John Pickering (1804),
removed for chronic intoxication and unhinged ranting
from the bench. Other officers of the United States who
lost their posts for erratic behavior include judges Mark
Delahay (1873), for habitual drunkenness, and George W.
English, whose arbitrary decrees and profane diatribes
tended "to excite fear and distrust" in the impartiality of his
court.[293]

There's *presidential* precedent available as well, from the
1868 impeachment of Andrew Johnson. The tenth article of

impeachment against Johnson charged the president with "a high misdemeanor in office" based on a series of "intemperate, inflammatory, and scandalous harangues" he'd delivered in an 1866 speaking tour. Those speeches, according to Article X, were "peculiarly indecent and unbecoming in the Chief Magistrate" and brought his office "into contempt, ridicule, and disgrace."[294]

Johnson, who'd been visibly drunk for his maiden speech as vice president, was supposedly sober during the Swing Around the Circle tour, during which he accused Congress of, among other things, "undertak[ing] to poison the minds of the American people" and having substantially planned a racial massacre in New Orleans that July. Much of the offending rhetoric cited in Article X wouldn't be considered particularly shocking today, but at the time it was a radical departure from prevailing norms of presidential conduct. Gen. Ulysses S. Grant, dragged along on the tour, wrote to his wife that "I have never been so tired of anything before as I have been with the political stump speeches of Mr. Johnson. I look upon them as a national disgrace."[295]

Article X, which never came to a vote in the Senate, was controversial at the time: some senators thought it was improper, even dangerous, to rest a charge solely on presidential speech.[296] But according to Representative Butler, the lead impeachment manager, the backlash against the president's speeches made impeachment possible because "they disgusted everybody."[297] As Jeffrey Tulis explains in his seminal work *The Rhetorical Presidency*, "Johnson's popular rhetoric violated virtually all of the nineteenth-century norms" surrounding presidential popular communication; "he stands as the stark exception to general practice in that century, so demagogic in his appeals to the people" that he resembled "a parody of popular leadership."[298] Johnson's behavior was, you might say, *not normal.*

Past practice can show us that impeachment for abnormal public conduct is constitutionally permissible; it can't tell us when we've reached the point where it's justified. That goes to the question of substantiality, to which there is no strictly legal answer. But, in the spirit of Professor Black's law-school hypotheticals, suppose President Trump's Twitter feed was significantly more disturbing than it already is—that he used it to hurl racial epithets and sexual insults at his political opponents, or, like former congressman Anthony Weiner, to send lurid snapshots of himself to admiring female fans. Surely, in theory at least, there must come a point where the president's public deportment is so inconsistent with what his office requires that he's judged constitutionally unfit to serve.[299]

Whether or not we've reached that point, it is a misconception to frame the issue, as Cohen does, in terms of Trump failing "the presidential test of moral leadership" or "lack[ing] the ethical and moral rectitude to be President of the United States."[300] In living memory, presidents have conducted themselves abominably in their personal relationships, lied us into war, and, in John Dean's memorable phrase, used "the available federal machinery to screw [their] political enemies." Ethical rectitude may not be their strong suit.

In a 2017 essay entertaining the idea of impeaching Trump for conduct unbecoming, the legal scholar Sanford Levinson describes Trump as having "blasphemed the American civil religion as set out in the Preamble or the Gettysburg Address or Martin Luther King's 'I Have a Dream' speech."[301] This sacerdotal orientation toward the office is notably absent from the *Federalist*, in which the president is described as a figure who will have "no particle of spiritual jurisdiction."[302]

It might be better to think of the president's role in more earthbound, businesslike terms. The chief executive officer of the federal government isn't our high priest or moral leader, but he has, in the corporate jargon, an "outward-facing role." Just as a CEO is the public face of the company, the president is the head of state in our system: the figure who, for better or for worse, represents us to the world. Americans have a right to demand some minimum standards of appropriate conduct.

OBSTRUCTION OF JUSTICE

With obstruction of justice, we enter more familiar territory. Representative Sherman had good reason to base his article of impeachment against President Trump on obstruction charges: it's one of the few areas where we have presidential precedent.

Sherman's article, he explained, was largely based on the first article of impeachment against President Nixon.[303] Passed by the House Judiciary Committee on July 27, 1974, that article accused Nixon of participating in a "plan designed to delay, impede, and obstruct the investigation" of the Watergate burglary. Article I passed 27–11, with 6 of the Committee's 17 Republicans crossing the aisle to support it. However, the smoking-gun tape—which had Nixon plotting to enlist the CIA in the cover-up—wasn't released until a week after the vote. Had it been available, the dissenting Republicans later affirmed, the vote on Article I would have been unanimous.[304]

Twenty-four years later, the full House voted to approve two articles of impeachment against Bill Clinton. Article II, passed by a vote of 221–212, charged that Clinton had "prevented, obstructed, and impeded the administration of justice . . . [in] a Federal civil rights action brought against him," the Paula Jones sexual harassment lawsuit. By a vote of 50–50, the Senate failed to convict on Article II, but, as University of Chicago law professors Daniel J. Hegel and Eric A. Posner observe, "at no point during the impeachment proceedings was there serious debate as to whether presidential obstruction could be an impeachable offense."[305] For example, in the House Judiciary Committee's report on the Clinton impeachment, the dissenting Democrats never denied that obstruction was, in principle, impeachable—they mainly argued that Clinton had not, in fact, obstructed justice.[306] Some Senators explained their vote to acquit in terms of substantiality: that although obstruction could, under certain circumstances, merit removal, the offense in this case was not a sufficient breach of the public trust to justify that penalty.[307]

Representative Sherman's article of impeachment charges President Trump with high crimes and misdemeanors for having "prevented, obstructed and impeded the administration of justice." The pattern of behavior supporting that conclusion includes pressuring then FBI director James Comey to stop the investigation of former National Security Adviser Michael Flynn, firing Comey after he refused, and publicly admitting "that the main reason for the termination was that the Director would not close or alter the investigation" into Russian involvement in the 2016 campaign.[308]

As Sherman pointed out to his colleagues when he first circulated the draft article, "a finding of 'High Crimes and Misdemeanors' does not require the violation of any particular criminal statute."[309] And yet, the public debate over the Comey firing has focused almost monomaniacally on whether Trump's actions violated federal obstruction of justice statutes, such as 18 U.S.C. §§ 1503, 1505, and 1512.[310] But as constitutional scholar Greg Weiner points out, "whether POTUS committed technical obstruction is an important point," but not the only, "or even the primary point."[311] In an impeachment proceeding, the key question isn't whether the president violated a particular criminal statute, but whether his conduct has made him unworthy of continued public trust. In its explanation of the first article of impeachment against Nixon, the 1974 Judiciary Committee Report states that the president's

> actions were contrary to his trust as President and unmindful of the solemn duties of his high office. It was this serious violation of Richard M. Nixon's constitutional obligations as president, *and not the fact that violations of Federal criminal statutes occurred,* that lies at the heart of Article I [emphasis added].[312]

If Sherman's article advances, it will be up to the House to decide whether Trump's case more closely resembles Nixon's or Clinton's. But one thing is clear: the fact that Trump, as president, had the legal right to fire James Comey is no defense to either the crime or the impeachable offense of obstruction.

In a January 2018 memo to special counsel Robert Mueller, President Trump's legal team argued that the Comey firing cannot serve as the basis for an obstruction charge because "a President can fire an FBI Director at any time and for any reason." Any impact that termination might have had on the FBI investigation "is simply an effect of the President's lawful exercise of his constitutional power and cannot constitute obstruction of justice here."[313] But an otherwise lawful act can constitute criminal obstruction if undertaken with corrupt intent.[314] It can also, regardless of criminal liability, constitute an impeachable offense.[315] Richard Nixon had the legal right to order the firing of special prosecutor Archibald Cox, and the House had a legal right to impeach him for it—and surely would have, had Nixon not resigned.[316]

ABUSE OF THE PARDON POWER

The president also has the legal right, under Article II, Section 2 of the Constitution, to "grant Reprieves and Pardons for Offences against the United States, except in cases of Impeachment." A *Washington Post* story published in July 2017 suggested that President Trump was contemplating using that power broadly. Trump, the *Post* reported, had "asked his advisers about his power to pardon aides, family members and even himself" in connection with the special counsel's Russia investigation.[317] Trump chimed in on Twitter, calling the story "FAKE NEWS," but noting "all agree the U.S. President has the complete power to pardon."[318]

The president's power to self-pardon is an open question, otherwise Trump's view that he has "the complete power to pardon" is pretty close.[319] Sanford Levinson has called the pardon power "Perhaps the most truly monarchical aspect of the presidency."[320]

There's little doubt Trump could issue broad prospective pardons for Donald Trump, Jr., Jared Kushner, Paul Manafort, Mike Flynn, and anyone else who might end up in Robert Mueller's crosshairs—and it would be perfectly legal. It could also serve as legitimate grounds for an impeachable offense.

The Framers were aware of the potential for abuse inherent in the sweeping pardon powers they'd devised for the president. And repeatedly, in the Convention and the ratification debates, they identified the proper remedy: impeachment.

At the Philadelphia Convention, when Edmund Randolph moved to exempt cases of treason, James Wilson retorted that "Pardon is necessary for cases of treason, and is best placed in the hands of the Executive. If he be himself a party to the guilt he can be impeached and prosecuted."[321] At the Pennsylvania ratifying convention later that year, one delegate addressed the objection that the president could pardon treasonous coconspirators by noting that "the President of the United States may be impeached before the Senate, and punished for his crimes."[322] And, at the Virginia ratifying convention, when George Mason warned that the president "may frequently pardon crimes which were advised by himself," James Madison replied that

> There is one security in this case
> to which gentlemen may not have
> adverted: if the President be con-
> nected, in any suspicious manner, with
> any person, and there be grounds to
> believe he will shelter him, the House of

> Representatives can impeach him; [and]
> they can remove him if found guilty.[323]

The hypotheticals described by Wilson and Madison involved *self-dealing* pardons, issued to shield the president's coconspirators—and the president himself—from legal jeopardy. When a president uses the pardon power to protect himself from punishment, or directly secure political and financial benefit, we have the clearest case for impeachment.

Recent cases of self-dealing pardons that might have justified impeachment include George H. W. Bush's pardons of top Iran-Contra figures, including former defense secretary Caspar Weinberger, and Bill Clinton's pardon of financier Marc Rich, a fugitive wanted on federal charges of tax evasion, fraud, and violating the U.S. trade embargo on Iran. The Iran-Contra pardons put an end to the independent counsel's investigation of the scandal and prevented a trial in which Bush himself would likely have been called to testify. Clinton's pardon of Marc Rich was at least as self-serving: it was almost certainly motivated by massive contributions Rich had arranged to the Clinton Library fund.[324]

University of Missouri law professor Frank Bowman suggests that Clinton could rightfully have been impeached for the Marc Rich pardon, which "amounted to an exercise of presidential power in response to poorly concealed bribes."[325] But, like the Iran-Contra pardons, the Rich pardon came at the very end of the president's tenure, when impeachment hardly seemed worth the effort.[326]

In contrast, Donald Trump's first controversial pardon came early. On August 25, 2017, Trump issued a presidential pardon to former Maricopa County, Arizona, sheriff Joe Arpaio, who had gained national notoriety for harsh and often unlawful tactics in pursuit of undocumented aliens. Arpaio had been convicted of criminal contempt for flagrant disregard of a federal court order to stop detaining people solely on suspicion of immigration status. Trump made an end-run around his own Justice Department, ignoring the guidelines set out by DOJ's Office of the Pardon Attorney in order to reward an unrepentant, serial abuser of power who happened to be a loyal political ally.[327] If, as Hamilton suggested in the *Federalist*, "humanity and good policy" are the ends the pardon power is supposed to serve, its exercise in this case served neither.[328]

By pardoning Arpaio, "Donald J. Trump has offered encouragement to others to disobey Federal court orders with which Donald J. Trump may disagree," Representative Cohen charged in the fourth of five articles of impeachment he introduced in November 2017.[329] Professor Bowman calls the Arpaio pardon Trump's "first verifiable impeachable offense." Bowman notes, correctly, that the Framers saw impeachment as a mechanism for "respond[ing] to misuse by the president of express or implied powers given him elsewhere in the document." Trump's use of the pardon power here "undercut the power of the judiciary to enforce the law against officials who believe they can violate it with impunity" and was "a transparent pander to a politician's political base."[330]

None of that clearly distinguishes the Arpaio pardon from other controversial pardons issued by past presidents, however. In December 1971, for example, President Nixon commuted labor leader Jimmy Hoffa's sentence for pension fraud and jury tampering. The move was designed to curry favor with the Teamsters in the run-up to the 1972 election and may even have involved a quid pro quo in the form of illegal campaign contributions.[331] Early in his first term, President Reagan pardoned two top FBI officials who'd been convicted of authorizing illegal break-ins as part of the Bureau's COINTELPRO domestic espionage program. As with the Arpaio pardon, those pardons could be expected to send a message to officials willing to violate the law, or, as one of the pardoned FBI men preferred to phrase it, to "do their job 100 percent."[332]

Of course, the fact that past presidents have gotten away with similar offenses doesn't legally prevent Congress from pursuing impeachment for pardon power abuse now. It does, however, suggest that recourse to the remedy is unlikely in the case of a single controversial pardon.

Still, presidents generally reserve their most controversial pardons for late in their tenure, when they feel safe from the political consequences. Trump's brazenness in issuing the Arpaio pardon less than eight months into his presidency revealed a very different orientation toward political risk. Trump "has become fixated on his ability to issue pardons," the *Washington Post* reported in June 2018, shortly before the president announced, via Twitter, that "I have the absolute right to PARDON myself."[333]

Trump's controversy-be-damned approach to the pardon power may lead him to overreach. And, as the Nixon Inquiry staff noted, "the cause for the removal of a President may be based on his entire course of conduct in office" when that conduct demonstrates "a tendency to subvert constitutional government."[334]

IMPEACHMENT FOR ILLEGAL WARMAKING

A central purpose of impeachment was thwarting "attempts to subvert the Constitution";[335] congressional control of the war power was one of that document's core guarantees. "In no part of the constitution is more wisdom to be found," Madison wrote in 1793, "than in the clause which confides the question of war or peace to the legislature, and not to the executive department."[336]

How far we've drifted from that wisdom is evident in our recent debates over war powers. In the summer of 2017, shortly after President Trump threatened North Korea with "fire, fury, and frankly power the likes of which this world has never seen," the *New Yorker's* Evan Osnos flew into Pyongyang for a series of interviews with top regime officials. In the article he filed, Osnos recounted an interesting exchange with Ri Yong Pil, an apparatchik from the North Korean Foreign Ministry:

After several more toasts, Ri loosened
his tie and shed his jacket. He had some
questions. "In your system, what is the
power of the President to launch a war?"
he asked. "Does the Congress have the
power to decide?"

A President can do a lot without
Congress, I said. Ri asked about the
nuclear codes. . . . [T]he President
can launch nukes largely on his own,
I said. "What about in your country?"
His answer was similar. "Our Supreme
Leader has absolute power to launch
a war."[337]

That President Trump thinks he enjoys the same power
has been clear since the start of his administration. Asked
in April 2017 whether the president was prepared to act
alone against Pyongyang, then White House press secretary Sean Spicer replied that the administration would
make sure Congress is notified, but "he's going to utilize
the powers under Article II of the Constitution."[338] In
September, after North Korea claimed to have successfully
tested a hydrogen bomb, a reporter asked Trump: "Will you
attack North Korea?" His response: "We'll see."[339]

"If he starts a war with North Korea without congressional approval," Rep. Ted Lieu (D-CA) declared after
Trump's "fire and fury" threat, "that would be grounds

for impeachment."[340] It ought to be, if anything is. Abuse of war powers was one of the grounds for removal discussed at the Constitutional Convention. "The propriety of impeachments was a favorite principle" for Virginia's Edmund Randolph because "the Executive will have great opportunities of abusing his power; particularly in time of war when the military force, and in some respects the public money will be in his hands."[341] Moreover, the first federal impeachment case, brought less than a decade after the Constitution's ratification, centered on charges of unauthorized warmaking. In 1797, the House impeached Tennessee Senator William Blount for conspiring to raise a private army for "a military hostile expedition" against Spanish-held Louisiana and Florida. That case has come to stand for the proposition that senators are not subject to impeachment, but the charges against Blount also reflect the Founding-era belief that improper arrogation of the war power was serious enough to merit the ultimate constitutional remedy.

In recent decades, presidents have done more than merely conspire: they've repeatedly waged war without authorization from Congress. And yet, to date, we've never managed to impeach one for it. There's no one reason for that failure, but congressional complicity in presidential warmaking has been an important factor. In his 1973 book *The Imperial Presidency*, historian Arthur Schlesinger Jr. observed that the growth of executive war power had been "as much a matter of congressional abdication as of presidential usurpation."[342] From the Cold War era on, Congress has served as the Imperial Presidency's enabler abroad, funding unauthorized wars and facilitating presidential adventurism through overbroad delegations of military power. Presidential impeachments are difficult to begin with; they've proven harder still when Congress itself is implicated in the constitutional subversion it's called upon to remedy.

The closest America ever came to impeaching a president for illegal warmaking was in 1974, when the House Judiciary Committee considered, and rejected, an article of impeachment based on President Nixon's secret bombing of Cambodia. Belief that "Congress shared the blame" for usurpation of its prerogatives was a key reason behind the effort's collapse.[343]

The secret bombing campaign began in March 1969, when Nixon ordered U.S. planes to target North Vietnamese base camps in Cambodian territory along the border with Vietnam. The campaign, which included nearly 4,000 sorties dropping more than 100,000 tons of bombs through May 1970, was code-named Operation Menu, with the various phases of the campaign going by the monikers "Breakfast," "Lunch," "Snack," "Dinner," and "Dessert." The high-altitude, indiscriminate bombing runs caused massive civilian casualties among Cambodian farmers.

The Nixon administration went to great lengths to shield the operation from public scrutiny: even the classified records of targets selected were falsified. Nixon

ordered the chairman of the Joint Chiefs of Staff not to
reveal the campaign to any member of Congress, and kept
the bombing secret even from his own Secretary of State,
William P. Rogers.[344]

The full story emerged in 1973, thanks in large part
to former Air Force major Hal Knight, a radar operator
who'd been ordered to burn mission records and substitute
false strike reports. Knight testified that when he'd asked
his commanding officer why, he was told it was in order
to hide the bombing from the Senate Foreign Relations
Committee.[345] No more than a handful of reliable members
of Congress—six or eight—were informed of the operation.
When the story went public, Nixon was unapologetic:
there had been no secrecy with regard to anyone who had
any right to know or need to know.

On July 1, 1973, when Congress voted to cut off funds for
bombing Cambodia, the Operation Menu campaign had
still not been formally acknowledged by the president.[346]
The cutoff, negotiated with the administration to avoid a
veto, gave the president until August 15 to end U.S. military
involvement.[347]

Among the articles of impeachment considered by the
House Judiciary Committee the following summer was
one charging that Nixon had "authorized, ordered, and
ratified the concealment from the Congress . . . the existence, scope and nature of American bombing operations
in Cambodia in derogation of the power of the Congress to

declare war."[348] By a vote of 26–12, the Committee decided not to report the article to the full House.

In his book *War and Responsibility: Constitutional Lessons of Vietnam and Its Aftermath*, John Hart Ely blames the Democratic Party leadership for scuttling the article: they realized that "a full inquiry would have demonstrated that a few prominent members of their party had known about the secret bombing at the time."[349] The Judiciary Committee report put it more diplomatically: "opponents of the Article concluded that, even if President Nixon usurped Congressional power, Congress shared the blame through acquiescence or ratification of his actions."[350]

As Charles Black saw it, that was the correct result: when Congress shares the blame for an illegal war, it lacks the moral authority to impeach the president for it. A long period of congressional acquiescence to presidential warmaking had made it difficult to establish "knowing wrongfulness" when presidents wage war without clear authorization, Black believed, and in the Cambodian case, "Congress, by postponing until August 15, 1973, the deadline for its ending, would seem to have come close to ratifying it. One is sailing very close to the wind when one says, 'You may do it till August 15, but it is an impeachable offense.'"[351]

That can't be right. Congressional complicity helps explain why Congress has proved reluctant to sanction the president for waging illegal wars—it hardly *justifies* that reluctance.

During the ratification debates, one of the main objections to the Senate as a trial court for impeachments was that senators would come to a presidential trial with unclean hands. For example, having ratified a ruinous treaty negotiated by the president, expecting them to impeach him for it "would constitute the senators their own judges."[352] Neither Hamilton nor Madison had entirely persuasive answers to this charge. Madison argued that those senators "who were not seduced would pronounce sentence against him," and rotation in office would bring in new members who didn't share the blame.[353] Hamilton suggested that senators who'd been misled would want to "punish the abuse of their confidence [and] vindicate their own authority. . . . We may thus far count upon their pride, if not their virtue," he wrote in *Federalist* 66.[354]

Thus far, that's not how it has worked out. But Black's argument transforms a possible defect in impeachment's structure into a moral obligation to give the president a pass. Far better to tolerate some hypocrisy on the part of the president's accusers than to take an essential constitutional safeguard off the table pending the emergence of a blameless Congress.

By 1974, Black had concluded that congressional abdication had infected war powers practice so thoroughly that "only a very extreme and not now visible case ought to bring the impeachment weapon into play as a sanction against presidential warlike activity." However, he pointed out that Congress could remedy past errors by setting out clear rules for presidential use of military force, and "if it did, then the president's violation of the congressional rules would be impeachable beyond a doubt."[355] He seemed to have in mind an amended War Powers Resolution, shorn of any ambiguity as to whether presidents can introduce U.S. forces into hostilities without prior authorization.

Short of comprehensive reform of the War Powers Resolution, however, Congress could draw a red line in an individual case. Rep. Walter Jones (R-NC), one of the House's most jealous guardians of Congress's power to declare war, proposed such a move in March 2012, when the Obama administration publicly debated airstrikes on Syria. Jones introduced a concurrent resolution "expressing the sense of Congress that the use of offensive military force by a President without prior and clear authorization of an Act of Congress constitutes an impeachable high crime and misdemeanor under Article II, Section 4 of the Constitution."[356]

By late 2017, with President Trump alternately indulging in juvenile name-calling and issuing stern threats to North Korea, Congress debated several measures to prevent him from starting a war. Lieu offered a bill to prohibit a first-use nuclear strike without a declaration of war expressly authorizing it, while several Democratic senators crafted a bill restricting the use of funds for military operations in North Korea without specific congressional authorization.[357] Unlike those measures, a concurrent resolution wouldn't be subject to a presidential veto. Should diplomacy with

North Korea fail, and a new round of saber-rattling commence, Congress could use that tool as a means to reassert its constitutional prerogatives. A preemptive declaration that unauthorized warmaking is an impeachable offense could serve as a warning to the president, and a precommitment device for Congress: a public pledge to take action in the sort of extreme and highly visible case where impeachment is clearly merited.

Conclusion

On September 8, 1787, as the Philadelphia Convention
neared its close, North Carolina's Hugh Williamson
observed that there was "more danger of too much lenity
than of too much rigour towards the President."[358] He was
more prescient than he could have known. The Framers
described impeachment as an indispensable remedy, but
in the 23 decades since ratification, we've all but dispensed
with it.[359]

Why have presidential impeachments been so rare?
One obvious cause is the high structural barrier to removal.
Article I, Section 3 stipulates that "no Person shall be
convicted without the Concurrence of two thirds of the
Members present." It's unlikely that the Framers fully
appreciated how much that provision would narrow the
path toward impeachment. As the legal scholar F. H.
Buckley explains:

> Until the very end of the Philadelphia
> Convention, the delegates had agreed
> that presidents might be removed by
> a simple majority of votes, either by
> the House or the Senate. The decisive
> move to a supermajoritarian require-
> ment came at the very end, from the
> Committee on Unfinished Parts, in its

draft on September 4. Thereafter, the delegates spent only five days debating the draft. They knew they were almost finished, and were impatient for the Convention to end. . . . The new requirement of a Senate supermajority passed without comment, seemingly unnoticed. And yet it was as fundamental a change as any in the new draft.[360]

The practical effect of that change, in conjunction with the rise of political parties, has been to make it almost impossible to convict a president of impeachable offenses. Coming anywhere close has required extraordinary historical circumstances: a post-Reconstruction Senate overwhelmingly dominated by one party in the trial of Andrew Johnson; the near-total collapse of Richard Nixon's support by mid-1974.

Our Constitution makes it hard—perhaps *too* hard—to remove a president. And yet, we've made it harder still by erecting barriers to impeachment nowhere to be found in the Constitution. Among those self-imposed restraints are the legal misconceptions challenged in this study, such as the notion that impeachment is reserved solely for grave, criminal abuses of official power. But cultural superstitions surrounding the remedy have been at least as significant a disincentive as legal error.

On the rare occasions when the "I-word" is invoked, Americans conjure up specters of wounded democracy and constitutional collapse. Pundits, pols, and professors describe impeachment as reversing an election and overturning the will of the people.[361] Impeachment isn't just a threat to democracy: leading public intellectuals view it as a menace to ordered liberty itself—a doomsday device that the Framers, in their perversity, wired into our Constitution.

"To cut short a president's term in office before it is finished," the *Los Angeles Times* warned in the wake of the Comey firing, "is to contravene the will of the people as expressed in the election—the most fundamental act of democracy—and should be done in only the rarest and most exceptional of cases."[362] Trump's copartisans went further: a successful impeachment effort would be tantamount to a "coup against a constitutionally elected president."[363] In that, they echoed President Clinton's defenders two decades ago. In the impeachment fight of the late '90s it was the Democrats crying "coup" on the House floor, with left-leaning law professors echoing the charge.[364]

When impeachment talk is in the air, normally sober and judicious scholars resort to violent hyperbole. Given "the deep wounding such a step must inflict on the country," Charles Black observed in his 1974 *Handbook*, we should only "approach it as one would approach high-risk major surgery."[365] "Truly the political equivalent of capital punishment," Laurence Tribe declaimed in 1998: allowing

Congress "to decapitate the executive branch in a single stroke."[366] It's worse than that, NYU's Ronald Dworkin insisted: "the power to impeach a president is *a constitutional nuclear weapon*" [emphasis added] that "gives politicians the means to shatter the most fundamental principles of our constitutional structure."[367] Such fears are radically overblown. Impeachment neither vandalizes democracy nor threatens constitutional crisis.

Presidential removal hardly overturns the will of the people or reverses the prior election. To do that, it would have to replace the president with his opponent in the previous election. But the Twelfth Amendment, which provided distinct ballots for president and vice president, and the Twenty-fifth Amendment, which gives the sitting president the power to nominate a vice president to fill a vacancy in the office, have all but ensured that any president who's removed will be replaced by a member of his own party.[368]

Still less does removal via impeachment constitute a coup. It's an abuse of language to liken a peaceful constitutional process to the violent seizure of power by a cabal.[369] As Judge Posner has observed, "it is the rare coup that installs the duly elected successor to the leader deposed."[370]

Moreover, if history is any guide, there's little justification for the fear that impeachment is especially destabilizing. Far from constituting a "long national nightmare," the Watergate era crisis of confidence in our institutions was actually good for the country. The real nightmare was what Nixon and his predecessors had been able to get away with for so long. Coming to terms with those abuses helped Americans demystify the presidency and institute necessary checks on executive power. During the Clinton impeachment fight, "government ticked along in its usual way through thirteen months of so-called crisis."[371] Despite claims of looming apocalypse, late '90s prosperity rolled on, the markets unperturbed by President Clinton's struggles.

Few, if any, of the Framers viewed the prospect of presidential impeachment with the unbridled horror common among intellectual leaders today. Putting a president on trial for high crimes and misdemeanors was, to be sure, a serious affair, never to be undertaken casually. In *Federalist* 65, Hamilton writes of "the awful discretion, which a court of impeachments must necessarily have, to doom [the accused] to honor or to infamy."[372] Still, he maintained, that discretion would be necessary, periodically, as "an essential check in the hands of [the legislative] body upon the encroachments of the executive."[373]

At the Philadelphia Convention, Massachusetts's Elbridge Gerry insisted: "A good magistrate will not fear [impeachments]. A bad one ought to be kept in fear of them."[374] "A man in public office who knows that there is no tribunal to punish him, may be ready to deviate from his duty," James Iredell observed during the ratification debate in North Carolina, "but if he knows there is a tribunal for that purpose, although he may be a man of no principle, the very terror of punishment will perhaps deter him."[375]

No lesser punishment is likely to do the job. The few successful censure resolutions against sitting presidents have mostly faded into obscurity.[376] But the ignominious distinction of getting impeached is central to the stories of the Johnson and Clinton presidencies—a permanent black mark on their legacies.

Impeachment's history suggests that the mere threat of the ultimate remedy can deter bad behavior by men in high places.[377] Even failed attempts at removal can help vindicate important constitutional norms.[378] In such cases, as Keith Whittington explains, "the critical audience for the impeachment is the other current and future federal officers who are being instructed on the proper bounds of acceptable political behavior. The actual removal of the impeached official is almost beside the point."[379]

But the terror of punishment will hardly deter if even proposing impeachment is taboo. Whatever one's assessment of the current president, the notion that impeachment is a constitutional nuclear weapon is unhealthy for our democracy. Over the last century, the American presidency has been transformed from a comparatively modest chief magistrate into the most powerful office in the world. And, as the power of the office has grown, our political culture has embraced a host of myths and superstitions ensuring that the holder of that office enjoys greater job protection than virtually any other American.[380]

Consider that most jobs in this country are employment-at-will; absent membership in a legally protected class, most of us can be fired for good reason, bad reason, or no reason at all. At the top of the corporate hierarchy, for-cause termination is the norm—CEOs can be cashiered for "moral turpitude," "unprofessional conduct," and the like.[381] Yet we've somehow managed to convince ourselves that the *one job* in America where you have to commit a felony to get fired is the one where you actually get nuclear weapons.

That is not how our system is supposed to work, it's not what our Constitution requires, and it's not what we should accept for an office as powerful and dangerous as the American presidency.

Notes

1. In 1843, the House briefly considered, and overwhelmingly rejected (84–127) a motion to initiate an impeachment inquiry against President John Tyler for, among other offenses, "corrupt abuse of the veto power." Asher C. Hinds, *Hinds' Precedents of the House of Representatives of the United States* (Washington: Government Printing Office, 1907), § 2398.

2. Katherine Connor Martin, "'I' Is for . . . Impeachment: The I-Word," May 24, 2017, https://blog.oxforddictionaries.com/2017/05/24/i-is-for-impeachment-the-i-word/.

3. A very rough estimate of the prevalence of impeachment talk can be gleaned from Lexis searches during the first six months of the last three presidential administrations. A query of the "Major Newspapers" database for "Bush" in the same sentence as the root word "impeach" (Bush /s impeach!) gets 98 hits, many of which refer to signs at public protests and some of which pull in references to the 1998 impeachment of President Clinton. A similar search for the first six months of President Obama's first term gets 193 hits, also heavily weighted toward protest signs at rallies, along with mentions of Illinois governor Rod Blagojevich's impeachment. Through the first six months of the current administration, "Trump /s impeach!" results in over 1,300 hits. (Searches were conducted on October 4, 2017.)

4. S. 65, 115th Cong. (January 9, 2017), https://www.congress.gov/bill/115th-congress/senate-bill/65.

5. "Congressman Nadler Resolution of Inquiry into Conflicts of Interest, Ethics Violations, and Russia Ties Voted Down in Party-Line Vote," press release, February 28, 2017, https://nadler.house.gov/press-release/congressman-nadler-resolution-inquiry-conflicts-interest-ethics-violations-and-russia.

6. Norman Solomon, "The Long Road to Impeach Trump Just Got Shorter," *Huffington Post*, February 10, 2017, https://www.huffingtonpost.com/norman-solomon/the-long-road-to-impeach_b_14674200.html.

7. Nadler's resolution went down on a party-line vote of the House Judiciary Committee, and Warren's bill never got a hearing.

Kyle Cheney, "House GOP Defeats Resolution Requesting Trump-Russia Documents," *Politico*, February 28, 2017.

8. *Fox & Friends*, Twitter, June 9, 2017, 8:18 a.m., https://twitter.com/foxandfriends/status/873167417232338949.

9. "Impeaching Donald John Trump, President of the United States, for High Crimes and Misdemeanors," H.R. Res. 438, 115th Cong. (July 12, 2017), https://www.congress.gov/bill/115th-congress/house-resolution/438/text.

10. "Congressman Sherman Introduces Article of Impeachment: Obstruction of Justice," press release, July 12, 2017, https://sherman.house.gov/media-center/press-releases/congressman-sherman-introduces-article-of-impeachment-obstruction-of.

11. Cristina Marcos, "House Democrat Introduces Bill to Amend Presidential Removal Procedures," *The Hill*, April 17, 2017, http://thehill.com/homenews/house/329206-house-democrat-introduces-bill-to-amend-presidential-removal-procedures.

12. "Ranking Member Cohen to Introduce Articles of Impeachment against President Donald Trump after Comments on Charlottesville," press release, August 17, 2017, https://cohen.house.gov/media-center/press-releases/ranking-member-cohen-introduce-articles-impeachment-against-president.

13. Cristina Marcos, "Dem Lawmaker Threatens to Force Trump Impeachment Vote Next Week," *The Hill*, September 26, 2017, http://thehill.com/blogs/floor-action/house/352456-dem-lawmaker-threatens-to-force-trump-impeachment-vote-next-week.

14. Trump's approval rating stood at 39.6 percent in the RealClearPolitics average on July 26, 2017: "President Trump Job Approval," *RealClearPolitics*, https://www.realclearpolitics.com/epolls/other/president_trump_job_approval-6179.html. Two July 2017 polls on support for impeachment put it at over 40 percent. See Susan Page and Emma Kinery, "Poll: Americans Split 42%-42% on Impeaching Trump," *USA Today*, July 24, 2017; and "Trump Rating Holds Steady Despite Campaign's 2016 Russia Meeting," Monmouth University Polling Institute, July 17, 2017, https://www.monmouth.edu/polling-institute/reports/MonmouthPoll_NJ_071717/.

15. Patrick Murray, "Public Opinion on Impeachment: Lessons from Watergate," June 12, 2017, http://monmouthpoll.blogspot.com/2017/06/public-opinion-on-impeachment-lessons.html.

16. *Federalist 65*, in George Carey and James McClellan, eds., *The Federalist* (Indianapolis: Liberty Fund, 2001), p. 338.

17. A Public Religion Research Institute poll released in August 2017 had 72 percent of Democrats supporting Trump's impeachment to just 7 percent of Republicans. Daniel Cox and Robert P. Jones, "Support for Impeachment Grows; Half of Americans Believe Russia Interfered with Election," PRRI.org, August 17, 2017, https://www.prri.org/research/poll-trump-russia-investigation-impeachment-republican-party/. A *USA Today*/iMediaEthics tally in late July 2017 put it at 58 percent of Democrats to 10 percent of Republicans. David W. Moore, "Public Evenly Divided over Impeachment of Donald Trump: *USA Today*/iMediaEthics Poll," iMediaEthics.org, July 24, 2017, https://www.imediaethics.org/imediaethics-usatoday-poll-public-divided-impeachment-donald-trump/.

18. Nick Berning, "MoveOn calls for Congress to Begin Impeachment Proceedings," June 8, 2017, https://front.moveon.org/moveon-calls-for-impeachment/#.WabaXtEpCfD.

19. Paula Jones filed her sexual harassment suit against Clinton after the *Spectator*'s exposé on "Troopergate"—Clinton's use of Arkansas state troopers to arrange sexual liaisons—mentioned her name. William E. Leuchtenburg, *The American President: From Teddy Roosevelt to Bill Clinton* (Oxford: Oxford University Press, 2015), p. 725.

20. William Murchison, "The Impeachment Delusion," *Spectator.org*, May 23, 2017, https://spectator.org/the-impeachment-delusion/.

21. Patrick Buchanan, "The Impeach-Trump Conspiracy," *RealClearPolitics*, June 9, 2017, https://www.realclearpolitics.com/articles/2017/06/09/the_impeach-trump_conspiracy_134146.html.

22. For a case that Ford's statement has been taken out of context, see Matthew J. Franck, "Ford, the Court, and Impeachment," *NationalReview.com*, December 28, 2006, http://www.nationalreview.com/bench-memos/51964/ford-court-and-impeachment-matthew-j-franck.

23. *Federalist 65*, in Carey and McClellan, eds., *The Federalist*, p. 338.

24. *Federalist 10*, in Carey and McClellan, eds., *The Federalist*, p. 43.

25. Charles L. Black, *Impeachment: A Handbook* (New Haven: Yale University Press, 1998), pp. 3–4.

26. Cass R. Sunstein, *Impeachment: A Citizen's Guide* (Cambridge: Harvard University Press, 2017), pp. 14–15. See also Statement of Laurence H. Tribe, "Background and History of Impeachment," Hearing before House Judiciary Committee, Subcommittee on the Constitution, November 9, 1998, http://www.law.jurist.org/wayback/tribe.htm: "Not knowing whose ox might be gored in the long run by an error in either direction, anyone who takes the task ahead with the seriousness its nature demands will necessarily proceed under what the philosopher John Rawls famously described as a veil of ignorance."

27. Sunstein suggests that you ask yourself: "Would I think the same thing if I loved the president's policies, and thought that he was otherwise doing a splendid job?" and "Would I think the same thing if I abhorred the president's policies, and thought that he was otherwise doing a horrific job?" Sunstein, *Impeachment: A Citizen's Guide*, p. 14.

28. See, for example, George Mason: "Some mode of displacing an unfit magistrate is rendered indispensable by the fallibility of those who choose, as well as by the corruptibility of the man chosen." Quoted in James McClellan and M. E. Bradford, eds., *Elliot's Debates, Vol. III: Debates in the Federal Convention of 1787* (Richmond: James River Press, 1989), p. 55; and James Madison, "indispensable that some provision should be made for defending the Community agst. the incapacity, negligence or perfidy of the chief Magistrate." Quoted in McClellan and Bradford, eds. *Elliot's Debates*, p. 317.

29. On Nixon as a "paradigmatic" case, see Michael J. Gerhardt, "Lessons of Impeachment History," *George Washington University Law Review* 67 (1999): 604.

30. Sunstein, *Impeachment: A Citizen's Guide*, p. 99.

31. McClellan and Bradford, eds., *Elliot's Debates*, p. 317.

32. House Judiciary Committee, "Constitutional Grounds for Presidential Impeachment: Report by the Staff of the Impeachment Inquiry," 93rd Cong., 2nd sess., 1974, pp. 17–18, 21 (hereinafter, "Nixon Inquiry Report").

33. *Federalist* 65, in Carey and McClellan, eds., *The Federalist*, p. 338.

34. "Nixon Inquiry Report," p. 21.

35. Jason J. Vicente, "Impeachment: A Constitutional Primer," Cato Institute Policy Analysis no. 318, September 18, 1998, p. 22.
36. *Federalist* 65, in Carey and McClellan, eds., *The Federalist*, p. 339.
37. "Impeachments, both colonial and English, were methods of bringing charges against men so close to the crown that indictment in the regular courts could not touch them." Peter Charles Hoffer and N. E. H. Hull, *Impeachment in America: 1635–1805* (New Haven: Yale University Press, 1984), p. 60.
38. Raoul Berger, *Impeachment: The Constitutional Problems* (Cambridge: Harvard University Press, 1973), p. 59. But see Clayton Roberts, "The Law of Impeachment in Stuart England: A Reply to Raoul Berger," *Yale Law Journal* 85 (June 1975): 1430–31, who dates the first use of the phrase to 1642.
39. "Nixon Inquiry Report," p. 5.
40. The period after the Restoration of Charles II in 1660 saw impeachments of Crown officials for such offenses as "negligent preparation for a Dutch invasion; loss of a ship through neglect to bring it to mooring," and "apply[ing] appropriated funds to public purposes other than those specified." Berger, *Impeachment: The Constitutional Problems*, pp. 68–69.
41. Joseph Story, *Commentaries on the Constitution of the United States*, vol. I, 5th ed. (Boston: Little, Brown, & Co., 1891), p. 585.
42. Hoffer and Hull, *Impeachment in America: 1635–1805*, p. 4.
43. Berger, *Impeachment: The Constitutional Problems*, p. 1.
44. Hoffer and Hull, *Impeachment in America: 1635–1805*, pp. 9–10.
45. Jack Simson Caird, "Impeachment," House of Commons Briefing Paper, June 6, 2016, p. 7, http://researchbriefings.parliament.uk/ResearchBriefing/Summary/CBP-7612: "The growth of the doctrine of collective cabinet responsibility, and the use of confidence motions have both contributed to the disuse of impeachments in modern times."
46. "Impeachments became increasingly direct in their intended challenge to Crown authority as the Revolution neared." Jonathan Turley, "Senate Trials and Factional Disputes: Impeachment as a Madisonian Device," *Duke Law Journal* 49 (October 1999): 23.
47. Hoffer and Hull, *Impeachment in America: 1635–1805*, p. 10: "In none of the early American cases does one find any attempt to justify the right of the colonial lower house to impeach. The right is taken as a given of English legislative jurisprudence."

48. Hoffer and Hull, *Impeachment in America: 1635–1805*, pp. 15–17: "There was no felony, but a palpable case for abuse of public power."

49. Hoffer and Hull, *Impeachment in America: 1635–1805*, p. 59.

50. Hoffer and Hull, *Impeachment in America: 1635–1805*, p. 54.

51. Hoffer and Hull, *Impeachment in America: 1635–1805*, p. 67.

52. Hoffer and Hull, *Impeachment in America: 1635–1805*, pp. 68–69.

53. Hoffer and Hull, *Impeachment in America: 1635–1805*, p. 61.

54. Michael J. Gerhardt, *The Federal Impeachment Process: A Constitutional and Historical Analysis* (Princeton: Princeton University Press, 1996), p. 4.

55. McClellan and Bradford, eds., *Elliot's Debates*, p. 309.

56. McClellan and Bradford, eds., *Elliot's Debates*, p. 316.

57. McClellan and Bradford, eds., *Elliot's Debates*, p. 316.

58. McClellan and Bradford, eds., *Elliot's Debates*, pp. 55, 314–20.

59. McClellan and Bradford, eds., *Elliot's Debates*, pp. 136–37.

60. See *Federalist 65*: "In Great Britain, it is the province of the house of commons to prefer the impeachment; and of the house of lords to decide upon it." In Carey and McClellan, eds., *The Federalist*, p. 339.

61. McClellan and Bradford, eds., *Elliot's Debates*, p. 573.

62. McClellan and Bradford, eds., *Elliot's Debates*, pp. 57, 136, 374, 464.

63. McClellan and Bradford, eds., *Elliot's Debates*, p. 572. Later that day, the delegates changed "agst. the State" to "against the United States." By September 12, the Committee on Style and Arrangement tightened the final draft to remove that phrase.

64. Jeffrey K. Tulis, "Impeachment in the Constitutional Order," in Joseph M. Bessette and Jeffrey K. Tulis, *The Constitutional Presidency* (Baltimore: Johns Hopkins University Press, 2009), pp. 241, 229.

65. Article I, Section 2, clause 5; Article I, Section 3, clause 6.

66. Article I, Section 3, clause 7.

67. Richard A. Posner, *An Affair of State: The Investigation, Impeachment, and Trial of President Clinton* (Cambridge: Harvard University Press, 1999), p. 98.

68. *Webster's American Dictionary of the English Language* (1828). See also Hoffer and Hull, *Impeachment in America: 1635–1805*, p. 102: "The addition of misdemeanors to the list of offenses meant that the House of Representatives was permitted to charge officials

with minor breaches of ethical conduct, misuse of power, and neglect of duty, as well as more prolonged egregious or financially rapacious misconduct."

69. James Wilson, *Collected Works of James Wilson*, ed. Kermit L. Hall and Mark David Hall, vol. 2 (Indianapolis: Liberty Fund, 2007), http://oll.libertyfund.org/titles/2074#Wilson_4141_459.

70. "Malversation," *Oxford English Dictionary*, https://en.oxforddictionaries.com/definition/malversation.

71. Hoffer and Hull, *Impeachment in America: 1635–1805*, p. 102. See also Forrest McDonald, "Background and History of Impeachment: Hearing Before the Subcommittee on the Constitution," November 9, 1998, pp. 216–17:

High crimes and misdemeanors had, according to the leading commentators, at least three different meanings. One was suggested by Sir William Blackstone's successor to the Viner lecturer at Oxford, Sir Richard Wooddeson, in his lengthy analysis of impeachment, namely that "high" meant crimes or misdemeanors of whatever seriousness committed by persons of a high station. The other readings turn upon whether the adjective "high" is meant to refer to both crimes and misdemeanors, or whether "high crimes" is one thing and "misdemeanors" is another. If the latter is to be understood, then the sense of the clause is that the president is impeachable for Treason, Bribery, or other high crimes, as well as for misdemeanors. In *Federalist* 69, indeed, that is Hamilton's reading—he says high crimes or misdemeanors. That is also the reading I would give it.

72. William Blackstone, *Commentaries on the Laws of England*, ed. William Carey Jones, vol. II (San Francisco: Bancroft-Whitney Co., 1916), p. 2295.

73. *Federalist 65*, in Carey and McClellan, eds., *The Federalist*, p. 339.

74. James Wilson, *Collected Works of James Wilson*, ed. Kermit L. Hall and Mark David Hall, vol. 1 (Indianapolis: Liberty Fund, 2007), http://oll.libertyfund.org/titles/2072#Wilson_4140_3091.

75. John O. McGinnis, "Impeachment: The Structural Understanding," *George Washington University Law Review* 67 (March 1999): 652.

76. "Nixon Inquiry Report," p. 17.

77. See Frank O. Bowman III and Stephen L. Sepinuck, "High Crimes and Misdemeanors: Defining the Constitutional Limits of

Presidential Impeachment," *California Law Review* 72 (Fall 1999): 1558–63.

78. Michael J. Klarman, "Constitutional Fetishism and the Clinton Impeachment Debate," *University of Virginia Law Review* 85, no. 4 (1999): 646.

79. Bowman and Sepinuck, "High Crimes and Misdemeanors," pp. 1522–23.

80. David P. Currie, *The Constitution in Congress: The Federalist Period, 1789–1801* (Chicago: University of Chicago Press, 1997), p. 3.

81. Senate Resolution on William Blount, July 4, 1797, Founders Online: https://founders.archives.gov/documents/Jefferson/01-29-02-0371.

82. Currie, *The Constitution in Congress: The Federalist Period, 1789–1801*, p. 276. Under Article I, Section 5, "Each House [of Congress] may determine the Rules of its proceedings, punish its members for disorderly behavior, and, with the concurrence of two-thirds, expel a member."

83. *Hinds' Precedents*, § 2302. Other charges included attempting to foment an attack on Spanish territory by the Cherokee and Creek nations and conspiring to "alienate the tribes from the President's [Indian] agent."

84. Jonathan Turley, "The Executive Function Theory, the Hamilton Affair, and Other Constitutional Mythologies," *North Carolina Law Review* 77 (1999): 1820.

85. Currie, *The Constitution in Congress: The Federalist Period, 1789–1801*, p. 281. For an argument that the Blount case didn't settle that question, see Buckner F. Melton, Jr., "Let Me Be Blunt: In *Blount*, the Senate Never Said that Senators Aren't Impeachable," *Quinnipiac Law Review* 33 (2014): 33–57.

86. *Hinds' Precedents*, § 2318.

87. Gordon S. Wood, *Empire of Liberty: A History of the Early Republic, 1789–1815* (Oxford: Oxford University Press, 2009), p. 420.

88. "Although Jefferson complained that impeachment was 'a *bungling way*' of dealing with the problem, he was reluctantly willing to give it a try." Wood, *Empire of Liberty*, p. 422.

89. David P. Currie, *The Constitution in Congress: The Jeffersonians, 1801–1829* (Chicago: University of Chicago Press, 2001), p. 23.

90. *Hinds' Precedents*, § 2328. Pickering had released the ship to its owner, a prominent Federalist, without hearing evidence that

the duties had been paid, and refused to allow the government to appeal the ruling.

91. *Hinds' Precedents*, § 2328.

92. For a critical view of the Pickering impeachment, see Lynn W. Turner, "The Impeachment of John Pickering," *American Historical Review* 54, no. 3 (April 1949): 485–507.

93. Indeed, the way the Republicans framed the vote reflected some unease about the insanity issue. Rejecting a Federalist proposal that the question take the form of whether Pickering was "guilty of high crimes and misdemeanors," they opted for the formulation "guilty as charged"—a means of "keeping out of sight the questions of law implied" in the constitutional standard, according to John Quincy Adams. Currie, *The Constitution in Congress: The Jeffersonians, 1801–1829*, pp. 26–27.

94. Currie, *The Constitution in Congress: The Jeffersonians, 1801–1829*, p. 28. Henry Adams, otherwise quite critical of the Republicans' behavior in the Pickering episode, acknowledges the strength of this argument: "If insanity or any other misfortune was to bar impeachment, the absurdity followed that unless a judge committed some indictable offence the people were powerless to protect themselves." Henry Adams, *History of the United States of America under the Administration of Thomas Jefferson* (New York: Charles Scribner's Sons, 1909), Kindle Edition, loc. 6481 of 21677.

95. Adams, *History of the United States of America under the Administration of Thomas Jefferson*, Kindle Edition, loc. 6393 of 21677.

96. William H. Rehnquist, *Grand Inquests: The Historic Impeachments of Justice Samuel Chase and President Andrew Johnson* (New York: William Morrow, 1992), pp. 104–5.

97. Thomas Jefferson, letter to Spencer Roane, September 6, 1819, http://press-pubs.uchicago.edu/founders/documents/a1_8_18s16.html.

98. Wood, *Empire of Liberty*, p. 424.

99. See William H. Rehnquist, *Grand Inquests*, p. 125: "Supreme Court justices sitting on circuit stopped including political harangues in their charges to grand juries."

100. Andrew Johnson, "Proclamation 134—Granting Amnesty to Participants in the Rebellion, with Certain Exceptions," May 29, 1865, American Presidency Project, http://www.presidency.ucsb.

edu/ws/index.php?pid=72392; and Andrew Johnson, "Proclamation 135—Reorganizing a Constitutional Government in North Carolina," May 29, 1865, American Presidency Project, http://www.presidency.ucsb.edu/ws/index.php?pid=72403.

101. "In North Carolina all of those able to vote before the Civil War and who fell within the scope of Johnson's pardons could vote. This formulation denied freedmen the franchise while granting it to men who had rebelled against the United States." Richard White, *The Republic for Which It Stands: The United States During Reconstruction and the Gilded Age, 1865–1896* (Oxford: Oxford University Press, 2017), p. 38.

102. David O. Stewart, *Impeached: the Trial of President Andrew Johnson and the Fight for Lincoln's Legacy* (New York: Simon & Schuster, 2009), Kindle Edition, p. 23.

103. Keith E. Whittington, "Bill Clinton Was No Andrew Johnson: Comparing Two Impeachments," *University of Pennsylvania Journal of Constitutional Law* 2 (March 2000): 426.

104. Michael Les Benedict, "From Our Archives: A New Look at the Impeachment of Andrew Johnson," *Political Science Quarterly* 113 (Autumn 1998): 495.

105. See Rehnquist, *Grand Inquests*, pp. 208–15.

106. Disagreements between the House and the Senate over whether Cabinet officers should be covered led to the adoption of compromise language that clouded the Act's application to Secretary of War Edwin M. Stanton. The act stipulated that cabinet members "shall hold their offices respectively for and during the term of the President by whom they may have been appointed and for one month thereafter, subject to removal by and with the advice and consent of the Senate." Stanton had been appointed by Lincoln; if, as Johnson's defense counsel would argue, "death is a limit," then Lincoln's term ended in April 1865 and the act's protections no longer applied to Stanton. See Stewart, *Impeached: the Trial of President Andrew Johnson and the Fight for Lincoln's Legacy*, p. 208.

107. 14 Stat. 432, § 9.

108. Berger, *Impeachment: The Constitutional Problems*, pp. 259–60.

109. Stewart, *Impeached: the Trial of President Andrew Johnson and the Fight for Lincoln's Legacy*, p. 156.

110. The articles of impeachment are available at United States Senate, "The Impeachment of Andrew Johnson (1868) President of the United States: Articles of Impeachment," https://www.senate.gov/artandhistory/history/common/briefing/Impeachment_Johnson.htm#7.

111. United States Senate, "The Impeachment of Andrew Johnson."

112. Rehnquist, *Grand Inquests*, p. 247.

113. Stewart concludes that "it is more likely than not" that some senators were paid off to acquit the president. Stewart, *Impeached: the Trial of President Andrew Johnson and the Fight for Lincoln's Legacy*, p. 295.

114. See Rehnquist, *Grand Inquests*, pp. 240–46; and Stewart, *Impeached: the Trial of President Andrew Johnson and the Fight for Lincoln's Legacy*, p. 317.

115. "'I Have Impeached Myself': Edited Transcript of David Frost's Interview with Richard Nixon Broadcast in May 1977," *Guardian*, September 7, 2007, https://www.theguardian.com/theguardian/2007/sep/07/greatinterviews1.

116. Michael E. Miller, "Like Trump, Nixon Was Obsessed with Leaks. It Led to Watergate—and Ruin," *Washington Post*, July 22, 2017, https://www.washingtonpost.com/news/retropolis/wp/2017/06/22/like-trump-nixon-was-obsessed-with-leaks-it-led-to-watergate-and-ruin/?utm_term=.1ee7091a09cc.

117. Andrew Kohut, "How the Watergate Crisis Eroded Public Support for Richard Nixon," PewResearch.org, August 8, 2014, http://www.pewresearch.org/fact-tank/2014/08/08/how-the-watergate-crisis-eroded-public-support-for-richard-nixon/.

118. *US v. Nixon*, 418 U.S. 683 (1974).

119. U.S. Congress, "Articles of Impeachment Adopted by the House of Representatives Committee on the Judiciary," July 27, 1974, American Presidency Project, http://www.presidency.ucsb.edu/ws/?pid=76082.

120. *Deschler's Precedents of the House of Representatives* (Washington: Government Printing Office), § 15.13.

121. U.S. Congress, "Articles of Impeachment," July 27, 1974.

122. U.S. Congress, "Articles of Impeachment," July 27, 1974.

123. House Judiciary Committee, "Impeachment of Richard M. Nixon, President of the United States," 93rd Cong., 2d sess., August 20,

1974, Report No. 93-1305, pp. 220–23. (Hereinafter referred to as "Nixon Judiciary Committee Report.")

124. "Nixon Judiciary Committee Report," pp. 217–19.

125. University of Virginia Miller Center, "The Smoking Gun," audio recording and transcript of Richard Nixon and Bob Haldeman, June 23, 1972, https://millercenter.org/the-presidency/educational-resources/the-smoking-gun.

126. Albin Krebs, "Notes on People," *New York Times*, June 5, 1973, http://www.nytimes.com/1973/06/05/archives/tango-stars-fined-notes-on-people.html?_r=0.

127. For background on the Independent Counsel Statute, see Benjamin J. Priester, Paul G. Roselle, and Mirah A. Horowitz, "The Independent Counsel Statute: A Legal History," *Law & Contemporary Problems* 62: (Winter 1999): 5–109.

128. Leuchtenburg, *The American President: From Teddy Roosevelt to Bill Clinton*, pp. 725, 768.

129. For a summary of the events leading to Clinton's impeachment, and the factual basis of the charges, see Posner, *An Affair of State*, pp. 16–58.

130. 28 U.S.C. § 595(c).

131. James E. Rogan, *Catching Our Flag: Behind the Scenes of a Presidential Impeachment* (Washington: WND Books, 2011), Kindle Edition, loc. 1648–1651 of 7042.

132. Rogan, *Catching Our Flag*, loc. 1364–65 of 7042.

133. "Impeaching William Jefferson Clinton, President of the United States, for High Crimes and Misdemeanors," H. Res. 611, 105th Cong., December 16, 1998, https://www.congress.gov/bill/105th-congress/house-resolution/611.

134. "Impeaching William Jefferson Clinton, President of the United States, for High Crimes and Misdemeanors."

135. House Judiciary Committee, "Impeachment of William Jefferson Clinton, President of the United States," 105th Cong., 2d sess., December 16, 1998, Report 105-830, pp. 118, 121–23. The vote margins were 205–229 on "Perjury in the Civil Case" and 148–205 on "Abuse of Power."

136. Richard Morin, "Approval of Congress Drops in Poll," *Washington Post*, October 12, 1998, http://www.washingtonpost.com/wp-srv/politics/special/clinton/stories/poll101298.htm.

137. Alison Mitchell and Eric Schmitt, "The 1998 Elections: Congress—the Overview; GOP in Scramble over Blame for Poor Showing at the Polls," *New York Times*, November 5, 1998, http://www.nytimes.com/1998/11/05/us/1998-elections-congress-overview-gop-scramble-over-blame-for-poor-showing-polls.html.

138. Jared P. Cole and Todd Garvey, *Impeachment and Removal*, CRS Report no. R44260 (Washington: Congressional Research Service, 2015), p. 1, https://fas.org/sgp/crs/misc/R44260.pdf.

139. "Nixon Inquiry Report," p. 50.

140. Cole and Garvey, *Impeachment and Removal*, p. 1; "List of Individuals Impeached by the House of Representatives," United States House of Representatives, http://history.house.gov/Institution/Impeachment/Impeachment-List/; and Sunstein, *Impeachment: A Citizen's Guide*, pp. 108–13.

141. Berger, *Impeachment: The Constitutional Problems*, p. 1.

142. "Nixon Inquiry Report," p. 17.

143. "Nixon Inquiry Report," p. 20.

144. *Nixon v. U.S.*, 506 U.S. 224 (1993); House Judiciary Committee, "Impeachment of G. Thomas Porteous, Jr., Judge of the United States District Court for the Eastern District of Louisiana," 111th Cong., 2d sess., March 4, 2010, H. Rept. no. 111–427.

145. *Hinds' Precedents*, § 2470.

146. *Hinds' Precedents*, § 2346.

147. *Hinds' Precedents*, § 2505. (Delahay resigned after impeachment and no trial was held in the Senate.)

148. Kent "engaged in conduct with respect to employees . . . incompatible with the trust and confidence placed in him as a judge," according to Articles I and II. House Judiciary Committee, "Impeachment of Judge Samuel B. Kent," 111th Congress, 1st sess., June 17, 2009, H. Rept., pp. 111–59. For more on the Kent case, see Skip Hollandsworth, "Perversion of Justice," *Texas Monthly*, December 2009, https://www.texasmonthly.com/articles/perversion-of-justice/.

149. "Impeachment Trials by the Senate," CQ Researcher, http://library.cqpress.com/cqresearcher/document.php?id=cqresrre1926041700#H2_6.

150. "Impeachment of Judge Ritter," *Deschler's Precedents of the House of Representatives* (Washington: Government Printing Office), 1994,

§ 18.7, https://www.gpo.gov/fdsys/pkg/gpo-hprec-deschlers-v3/pdf/gpo-hprec-deschlers-v3-5-5-5.pdf.

151. See, for example, Bowman and Sepinuck, "High Crimes and Misdemeanors," p. 1535.

152. Statement of Cass Sunstein, "Background and History of Impeachment," Hearing before House Judiciary Committee, Subcommittee on the Constitution, November 9, 1998, in "Impeachment of President William Jefferson Clinton: The Evidentiary Record Pursuant to S. Res. 16," 106th Cong., 1st sess., January 8, 1999, p. 89.

153. Akhil Amar, "Foreword," in Black, *Impeachment: A Handbook* (1998 ed.), p. xi.

154. Cass R. Sunstein, "Impeaching the President," *University of Pennsylvania Law Review* 147 (December 1998): 304. See also Gerhardt, *The Federal Impeachment Process*, pp. 83–85.

155. Mike Lillis, "Pelosi: No Grounds for Impeaching Trump," *The Hill*, February 6, 2017, http://thehill.com/homenews/house/318075-pelosi-no-grounds-for-impeaching-trump.

156. Story, *Commentaries on the Constitution of the United States*, p. 580.

157. Sara Sun Beale, "Federalizing Crime: Assessing the Impact on the Federal Courts," *Annals of the American Academy of Political and Social Science* 543 (January 1996): 40, https://scholarship.law.duke.edu/cgi/viewcontent.cgi?referer=&httpsredir=1&article=2045&context=faculty_scholarship.

158. Story, *Commentaries on the Constitution of the United States*, p. 583.

159. Cole and Garvey, *Impeachment and Removal*, p. 9.

160. Cass R. Sunstein, "Impeaching the President," p. 291.

161. Gerhardt, *The Federal Impeachment Process*, p. 103.

162. See Bowman and Sepinuck, "High Crimes and Misdemeanors," p. 1559: "In the case of impeachment, two of the four conventionally articulated rationales for criminal prosecution and punishment—retribution, rehabilitation, deterrence, and incapacitation—are absent. The goal of impeachment is neither retribution against, nor rehabilitation of, the official who commits an offense." See also Greg Weiner, "Impeachment's Political Heart," *New York Times*, May 18, 2017: "The purpose of impeachment is not punitive. It is prophylactic."

163. U.S. Constitution, Article I, Section 3, clause 7.

164. Story, *Commentaries on the Constitution of the United States*, pp. 586–87.

165. Berger, *Impeachment: The Constitutional Problems*, p. 85.

166. *Johnson's English Dictionary* (Boston: Cottons and Barnard, 1834), p. 693.

167. "Nixon Inquiry Report," pp. 26–27.

168. Black, *Impeachment: A Handbook*, p. 49. See also Gerhardt, *The Federal Impeachment Process*, p. 177: "Constitutional law explicates what is permissible, but politics dictates what should be done . . . simply because some course of action is constitutional does not necessarily mean that such an undertaking is either prudent or mandatory."

169. "Congressman Sherman Introduces Article of Impeachment: Obstruction of Justice."

170. McClellan and Bradford, eds., *Elliot's Debates*, p. 49.

171 McClellan and Bradford, eds., *Elliot's Debates*, p. 317.

172. McClellan and Bradford, eds., *Elliot's Debates*, p. 317.

173. McClellan and Bradford, eds., *Elliot's Debates*, p. 320.

174. Hoffer and Hull, *Impeachment in America: 1635–1805*, p. 219.

175. As noted above, Delahay, like Pickering, lost his post by being habitually "intoxicated off the bench as well as on the bench." Judge English demonstrated mental instability by dragging local officials into court in a nonexistent case, ranting at them, and threatening to remove them from office.

176. In practice, Section 3 has served as the Constitution's "Colonoscopy Clause," having been formally invoked three times for the procedure. See John Woolley and Gerhard Peters, "List of Vice-Presidents Who Served as 'Acting' President Under the 25th Amendment," American Presidency Project, http://www.presidency.ucsb.edu/acting_presidents.php.

177. U.S. Constitution, Twenty-fifth Amendment, Section 4.

178. Laurence Tribe, Twitter, January 21, 2017, 8:52 p.m., https://twitter.com/tribelaw/status/822985280189792256; and Laurence Tribe, Twitter, February 18, 2017, 3:40 p.m., https://twitter.com/tribelaw/status/833053570505273345. More recently, however, Tribe seems to have concluded it's an "impractical" solution. Laurence Tribe, Twitter, August 13, 2017, 9:03 a.m., https://twitter.com/tribelaw/status/896734018334490624.

179. Ross Douthat, "The 25th Amendment Solution for Removing Trump," *New York Times*, May 16, 2017, https://www.nytimes.com/2017/05/16/opinion/25th-amendment-trump.html.

180. Marcos, "House Democrat Introduces Bill to Amend Presidential Removal Procedures."

181. "Strengthening and Clarifying the 25th Amendment Act of 2017," H.R. 2093, 115th Cong., April 14, 2017, https://www.congress.gov/bill/115th-congress/house-bill/2093/text.

182. "Oversight Commission on Presidential Capacity Act," H.R. 1987, 115th Cong., April 6, 2017, https://www.congress.gov/bill/115th-congress/house-bill/1987/cosponsors?r=48.

183. Oversight Commission on Presidential Capacity Act, §§ 3(b); 5(d).

184. Oversight Commission on Presidential Capacity Act, § 6(b).

185. See Maria A. Oquendo, "The Goldwater Rule: Why Breaking It Is Unethical and Irresponsible," *American Psychiatric Association*, August 3, 2016, https://www.psychiatry.org/news-room/apa-blogs/apa-blog/2016/08/the-goldwater-rule.

186. 111 Cong. Rec. S15586 (daily ed., July 6, 1965) (statement of Sen. McCarthy).

187. Brian Kalt, *Constitutional Cliffhangers: A Legal Guide for Presidents and Their Enemies* (New Haven: Yale University Press, 2012), Kindle Edition, p. 1.

188. U.S. Constitution, Twenty-fifth Amendment, Section 4.

189 Kalt, *Constitutional Cliffhangers*, p. 61.

190. Kalt, *Constitutional Cliffhangers*, pp. 64–66.

191. Eric Posner, "Trump Could be Removed for Political Incompetence—Using the 25th Amendment," *Washington Post*, September 12, 2017, https://www.washingtonpost.com/opinions/trump-could-be-removed-for-political-incompetence--using-the-25th-amendment/2017/09/12/b6c62380-9718-11e7-82e4-f1076f6d6152_story.html?utm_term=.8d1cb5645446.

192. James Reston, "Why America Weeps," *New York Times*, November 23, 1963, http://www.nytimes.com/1963/11/23/why-america-weeps-kennedy-victim-of-violent-streak-he-sought-to-curb-in-the-nation.html?pagewanted=all.

193. John D. Feerick, *The Twenty-Fifth Amendment: Its Complete History and Applications*, 3rd ed. (New York: Fordham University Press, 2014), pp. 115–16.

194. Quoted in Eric M. Freedman, "The Law as King and the King as Law: Is a President Immune from Criminal Prosecution Before Impeachment?," *Hastings Constitutional Law Quarterly* 20 (1992): 56.

195. Feerick, *Twenty-Fifth Amendment*, p. 117. Rep. Richard H. Poff (R-VA), a key figure in the House debates, described the circumstances under which resort to Section 4 would be appropriate: "one is the case when the President by reason of some physical ailment or some sudden accident is unconscious or paralyzed. . . . The other is the case when the President, by reason of mental debility, is unable or unwilling to make any rational decision, including particularly the decision to stand aside." Feerick, *Twenty-Fifth Amendment*, p. 97.

196. Douthat, "The 25th Amendment Solution for Removing Trump."

197. Quoted in Turley, "Executive Function Theory," p. 1804. See also Sunstein, "Impeaching the President," pp. 288–89, arguing that the rejection of "maladministration" suggests "the Framers were thinking, exclusively or principally, of large-scale abuses of distinctly public authority."

198. Black, *Impeachment: A Handbook*, p. 29.

199. Turley, "Executive Function Theory," p. 1805.

200. McClellan and Bradford, eds., *Elliot's Debates*, p. 572.

201. As Joseph M. Bessette and Gary J. Schmitt noted, "the secrecy of the Convention's proceedings meant that [this exchange] was not known to the delegates in the state ratifying conventions [and] at least some of them seemed to have believed that 'high crimes and misdemeanors' was equivalent to Mason's rejected formulation." Joseph M. Bessette and Gary J. Schmitt, *What Does 'High Crimes and Misdemeanors' Mean?* (Claremont, CA: Henry Salvatori Center, Claremont McKenna College, 1998), https://www.cmc.edu/salvatori/publications/impeachment-essay.

202. "Nixon Inquiry Report," p. 6.

203. Jonathan Elliot, *The Debates in the Several State Conventions of the Adoption of the Federal Constitution*, vol. 3 (Virginia) [1827], Liberty Fund, http://oll.libertyfund.org/titles/1907#Elliot_1314-03_1060.

204. Story, *Commentaries on the Constitution of the United States*, p. 559.

205. Black, *Impeachment: A Handbook*, p. 33.

206. Cass Sunstein, who takes a narrow, abuse-of-power approach to impeachment's constitutional scope, acknowledges that

"neglecting constitutional duties" egregiously can be an impeachable offense. See Sunstein, *Impeachment: A Citizen's Guide*, p. 121.

207. Currie, *The Constitution in Congress: The Federalist Period, 1789–1801*, pp. 36–40.
208. James Madison, "Removal Power of the President," June 17, 1789, Founders Online, National Archives, http://founders.archives.gov/documents/Madison/01-12-02-0143. (Original source: *The Papers of James Madison*, ed. Charles F. Hobson and Robert A. Rutland, vol. 12 (Charlottesville: University Press of Virginia, 1979), pp. 232–239.
209. Although, as David Currie points out, "there was no consensus as to whether [the president] got that authority from Congress or the Constitution itself." Currie, *The Constitution in Congress: The Federalist Period, 1789–1801*, p. 41.
210. Philip Carter, "Articles of Impeachment for Donald J. Trump," *Slate*, May 16, 2017, http://www.slate.com/articles/news_and _politics/jurisprudence/2017/05/here_is_a_draft_of_articles_of_ impeachment_for_donald_j_trump.html.
211. See, for example, Christopher Fonzone and Joshua A. Geltzer, "Can President Trump Just Leave Key Executive Branch Offices Unfilled?," *Lawfare.com*, July 5, 2017, https://www.lawfareblog.com/can-president-trump-just-leave-key-executive-branch-offices -unfilled.
212. Carter, "Articles of Impeachment for Donald J. Trump."
213. "Partnership for Public Service Addresses Management Challenges and Opportunities for President Donald Trump at the 200 Day Mark," Partnership for Public Service, August 7, 2017, https://ourpublicservice.org/publications/viewcontentdetails. php?id=1953.
214. Philip Bump, "Trump Is Blaming Democrats for His Own Failure on Nominations," *Washington Post*, June 5, 2017, https://www. washingtonpost.com/news/politics/wp/2017/06/05/trumps -blaming-democrats-for-his-own-failure-on-nominations/?tid= a_inl&utm_term=.c469850387e8.
215. Cody Derespina, "Trump: No Plans to Fill 'Unnecessary' Appointed Positions," FoxNews.com, February 28, 2017, http:// www.foxnews.com/politics/2017/02/28/trump-no-plans-to-fill -unnecessary-appointed-positions.html.

216. Eric Lipton and Danielle Ivory, "Trump Says His Regulatory Rollback Already Is the 'Most Far-Reaching,'" *New York Times*, December 14, 2017, https://www.nytimes.com/2017/12/14/us/ politics/trump-federal-regulations.html.

217. See Alan Levin and Jesse Hamilton, "Trump Takes Credit for Killing Hundreds of Regulations That Were Already Dead," *Bloomberg Businessweek*, December 11, 2017, https://www. bloomberg.com/news/features/2017-12-11/trump-takes-credit -for-killing-hundreds-of-regulations-that-were-already-dead.

218. See "10 Executives Reshaping Government," *Government Executive*, January 23, 2018, https://www.govexec.com/cards /10-executives-reshaping-government/.

219. Ashley Parker, "'Ready, Shoot, Aim': President Trump's Loyalty Tests Cause Hiring Headaches," *Washington Post*, April 29, 2018, https://www.washingtonpost.com/politics/ready-shoo t-aim-president-trumps-loyalty-tests-cause-hiring-headaches/ 2018/04/29/7756ec9c-4a33-11e8-827e-190efaf1f1ee_story.html.

220. Black, *Impeachment: A Handbook*, p. 30.

221. Kevin O' Brien, "A Bureaucracy So Big that It Gets to Run Itself Is Dangerous," *Cleveland Plain-Dealer*, June 13, 2013, http://www. cleveland.com/obrien/index.ssf/2013/06/a_bureaucracy_so_big _that_it_h.html.

222. See, for example, Charles C.W. Cooke, "Obama: I'm Not Incompetent, Government Is," *National Review*, December 6, 2013, http://www.nationalreview.com/corner/365667.

223. Cynthia R. Farina, "False Comfort and Impossible Promises: Uncertainty, Information Overload, and the Unitary Executive," *University of Pennsylvania Journal of Constitutional Law* 12 (February 2010): 360, 410.

224. In the BP case, for example, some pointed to remote-controlled blowout preventers, mandated in Norway and Brazil, though not in the United States. Russell Gold, Ben Casselman, and Guy Chazan, "Leaking Oil Well Lacked Safeguard Device," *Wall Street Journal*, April 28, 2010, https://www.wsj.com/articles/SB100014240 52748704423504575212031417936798.

225. A Lexis search of major newspapers during the period of the spill (April 20, 2010 to September 19, 2010) turns up one reference to impeachment in the same paragraph as "Obama" and "BP," in a *Newark Star-Ledger* "Reader Forum": "Can you imagine had this

event occurred in the prior administration just how ferocious would be calls for President George Bush's impeachment . . . ?" "Reader Forum," *Newark Star-Ledger*, May 28, 2010.

226. "Impeaching George W. Bush, President of the United States, of High Crimes and Misdemeanors," H. Res. 1258, https://www.congress.gov/bill/110th-congress/house-resolution/1258.

227. Black, *Impeachment: A Handbook*, p. 46.

228. See American Law Institute, "Model Penal Code," § 2.02(2), "Kinds of Culpability Defined": 2(c) "Recklessly" and 2(d) "Negligently."

229. Black, *Impeachment: A Handbook*, p. 47.

230. Senator Bob Corker, Twitter, October 8, 2017, 10:13 a.m., https://twitter.com/SenBobCorker/status/917045348820049920.

231. Jonathan Martin and Mark Landler, "Bob Corker Says Trump's Recklessness Threatens 'World War III,'" *New York Times*, October 8, 2017, https://www.nytimes.com/2017/10/08/us/politics/trump-corker.html?_r=0.

232. Daniel W. Drezner, "White House Aides Can't Stop Talking about President Trump Like He's a Toddler [UPDATED]," *WashingtonPost.com*, August 21, 2017, https://www.washingtonpost.com/news/posteverything/wp/2017/08/21/the-trump-as-toddler-thread-explained-and-curated/?utm_term=.bb016279f658.

233. Carol E. Lee, Kristen Welker, Stefanie Ruhle, and Dafna Linzer, "Tillerson's Fury at Trump Required an Intervention from Pence," *NBC News*, October 4, 2017, https://www.nbcnews.com/politics/white-house/tillerson-s-fury-trump-required-intervention-pence-n806451.

234. Greg Miller and Greg Jaffe, "Trump Revealed Highly Classified Information to Russian Foreign Minister and Ambassador," *Washington Post*, May 15, 2017, https://www.washingtonpost.com/world/national-security/trump-revealed-highly-classified-information-to-russian-foreign-minister-and-ambassador/2017/05/15/530c172a-3960-11e7-9e48-c4f199710b69_story.html?utm_term=.c89c732a7cfc.

235. Keith Whittington, "Possibly Impeachable Offenses: The Need for Congressional Investigation," August 2, 2017, https://niskanencenter.org/blog/possibly-impeachable-offenses/.

236. McClellan and Bradford, eds., *Elliot's Debates*, p. 317.

237. Peter Baker and John F. Harris, "Clinton Admits to Lewinsky Relationship, Challenges Starr to End Personal 'Prying,'" *Washington Post*, August 18, 1998, https://www.washingtonpost.com/wp-srv/politics/special/clinton/stories/clinton081898.htm.

238. Jonathan Turley has dubbed this the "executive function theory" of impeachment. Turley, "Executive Function Theory," p. 1796.

239. Bernard J. Hibbitts, "More Than 430 Law Professors Send Letter to Congress Opposing Impeachment," *Jurist.org*, http://www.law.jurist.org/wayback/petit1.htm.

240. Sunstein, "Impeaching the President," pp. 313–14. Recently, Sunstein seems to have backed away from this claim somewhat, acknowledging that it seems "a bit nuts" to say that you couldn't impeach a president for a private murder. Ryan Goodman, "Q&A with Cass Sunstein on 'Impeachment: A Citizen's Guide,'" *JustSecurity.org*, October 23, 2017, https://www.justsecurity.org/46205/qa-cass-sunstein-impeachment-citizens-guide/.

241. Statement of Laurence H. Tribe, "Background and History of Impeachment."

242. Bernard J. Hibbitts, "More Than 430 Law Professors Send Letter to Congress Opposing Impeachment."

243. "Historians' Statement on Impeachment," *Washington Post*, October 28, 1998, http://www.washingtonpost.com/wp-srv/politics/special/clinton/stories/petition102898.htm; and John F. Harris, "400 Historians Denounce Impeachment," *Washington Post*, October 29, 1998, https://www.washingtonpost.com/archive/politics/1998/10/29/400-historians-denounce-impeachment/b2c18409-e033-44ee-9258-6215c12e22d3/?utm_term=.bdcfab90f78.

244. Black, *Impeachment: A Handbook*, pp. 3–4.

245. Hoffer and Hull, *Impeachment in America: 1635–1805*, p. 157.

246. Judge Halsted Ritter (1936) was removed on the grounds that he'd brought his court "into scandal and disrepute" through income tax evasion and accepting "substantial gifts from wealthy residents of his district, notwithstanding they had no cases pending before him." Berger, *Impeachment: The Constitutional Problems*, p. 93.

247. Turley, "Executive Function Theory," p. 1831. Other judicial impeachments for nonofficial conduct include Judge Harry E. Claiborne (1986) (income tax fraud) and Judge Walter Nixon (1989) (perjury).

248. Posner, *Affair of State*, p. 109.

249. Posner, *Affair of State*, pp. 105, 172.

250. Black, *Impeachment: A Handbook*, p. 39.

251. Allan J. Lichtman, *The Case for Impeachment* (New York: Harper Collins, 2017), p. 60.

252. "U Researcher: Trump University Lawsuits Present Potential Impeachment Case," *UNEWS* (University of Utah), September 20, 2016, https://unews.utah.edu/university-of-utah-researcher -trump-university-lawsuits-lay-groundwork-for-potential-impe achment-of-donald-trump/.

253. Christopher L. Peterson, "Trump University and Presidential Impeachment," *Oregon Law Review* 96 (2017): 57–121, Social Science Research Network, September 21, 2016, https://papers. ssrn.com/sol3/papers.cfm?abstract_id=2841306.254. Written Statement of Michael J. Gerhardt, Samuel Ashe Distinguished Professor of Constitutional Law, UNC–Chapel Hill School of Law, Committee on the Judiciary Task Force on the Possible Impeachment of Judge G. Thomas Porteous, Jr., December 15, 2009, p. 4, https://judiciary.house.gov/_files/hearings/pdf/ Gerhardt091215.pdf.

255. Another case arguably resting on prior conduct was that of Judge Archbald (1913). Five of the 13 articles of impeachment focused on improprieties committed in his previous position as a district court judge. See "Nixon Inquiry Report," p. 52. He escaped conviction on those charges, but the Senate found him guilty on the "catch-all" Article 13, which incorporated them. See Patrick J. McGinnis, "A Case of Judicial Misconduct: The Impeachment and Trial of Robert W. Archbald," *Pennsylvania Magazine of History and Biography* 101, no. 4 (October 1977): 506–20.

256. Michael A. Memoli, "Senate Convicts Louisiana Federal Judge in Impeachment Trial," *Los Angeles Times*, December 9, 2010, http:// articles.latimes.com/2010/dec/09/news/la-pn-senate -impeachment-20101209.

257. Noah Feldman and Jacob Weisberg, "What Are Impeachable Offenses?," *New York Review of Books*, September 28, 2017, http:// www.nybooks.com/articles/2017/09/28/donald-trump -impeachable-offenses/.

258. McClellan and Bradford, eds., *Elliot's Debates*, p. 317. Gouverneur Morris offered "corrupting his electors" as a sound basis for a

president's impeachment. McClellan and Bradford, eds., *Elliot's Debates*, p. 320.

259. House Judiciary Committee, "Impeachment of G. Thomas Porteous, Jr."

260. John A. Farrell, "When a Candidate Conspired With a Foreign Power to Win an Election," *Politico Magazine*, August 6, 2017, http://www.politico.com/magazine/story/2017/08/06/nixon-vietnam -candidate-conspired-with-foreign-power-win-election-215461.

261. Peter Baker, "Nixon Tried to Spoil Johnson's Vietnam Peace Talks in '68, Notes Show," *New York Times*, January 2, 2017; and John A. Farrell, "Nixon's Vietnam Treachery," *New York Times*, December 31, 2016.

262. Gerhardt, *The Federal Impeachment Process*, p. 109.

263. Hansi Lo Wang, "Lawsuit Could Put Trump's Sexual Misconduct Accusers Back in Spotlight," NPR.org, December 5, 2017, https:// www.npr.org/2017/12/05/568618889/lawsuit-could-put-trumps -sexual-misconduct-accusers-back-in-spotlight.

264. Norman L. Eisen and Richard Painter, "Trump Could Be in Violation of the Constitution His First Day in Office," *Atlantic*, December 7, 2016, https://www.theatlantic.com/politics/ archive/2016/12/trump-could-be-in-violation-of -the-constitution-his-first-day-in-office/509810/. See also Mark Joseph Stern, "High Crimes and Misdemeanors: Donald Trump Appears Determined to Violate the Constitution on Day One of His Presidency," *Slate*, January 4, 2017, http://www.slate.com/ articles/news_and_politics/jurisprudence/2017/01/donald_trump_ appears_determined_to_violate_the_constitution_on_day_one. html.

265. Norman L. Eisen, Richard Painter, and Laurence H. Tribe, "The Emoluments Clause: Its Text, Meaning, and Application to Donald J. Trump," Brookings Institution, December 16, 2016, pp. 21–22, https://www.brookings.edu/wp-content/uploads/2016/12/ gs_121616_emoluments-clause1.pdf. Actually, Eisen et al. maintain that Trump's children would *also* have to relinquish all ownership in Trump properties to cure the alleged violation of the Foreign Emoluments Clause.

266. James Cleith Phillips and Sara White, "The Meaning of the Three Emoluments Clauses in the U.S. Constitution: A Corpus Linguistic Analysis of American English, 1760–1799," *South Texas Law Review*

59 (2018): 37; Amandeep S. Grewal, "The Foreign Emoluments Clause and the Chief Executive," *Minnesota Law Review* 102 (2017): 641–42;

John Mikhail, "The Definition of 'Emolument' in English Language and Legal Dictionaries, 1523–1806," July 13, 2017, p. 15, http://dx.doi.org/10.2139/ssrn.2995693; and Robert G. Natelson, "The Original Meaning of 'Emoluments' in the Constitution," *Georgia Law Review* 52 (Fall 2017): 53. "During the founding era, there were at least four different meanings of 'emolument' current in official government discourse."

267. Eisen et al., "The Emoluments Clause," p.11; Eisen and Painter, "Trump Could Be in Violation of the Constitution His First Day in Office."

268. Eisen et al., "Emoluments Clause," pp. 11, 18.

269. There is also a credible argument, advanced by Seth Barrett Tillman, that the Foreign Emoluments Clause does not apply to the president on the grounds that the language "Office of Profit or Trust under [the United States]" applies only to "holders of appointed federal statutory offices, not elected or constitutionally created positions" such as the presidency. Seth Barrett Tillman, "The Original Public Meaning of the Foreign Emoluments Clause: A Reply to Professor Zephyr Teachout," *Northwestern University Law Review Colloquy* 107 (2013): 181–82.

270. Article II, Section I, clause 7. An alternative taxonomy designates this as the "Presidential Emoluments Clause." See Phillips and White, "The Meaning of the Three Emoluments Clauses in the U.S. Constitution," pp. 44–45.

271. Andy Grewal, "Should Congress Impeach Obama for His Emoluments Clause Violations?" *Notice & Comment* (blog), December 13, 2016, http://yalejreg.com/nc/should-congres s-impeach-obama-for-his-emoluments-clause-violations/.

272. Natelson, "The Original Meaning of 'Emoluments,'" pp. 48–49.

273. Gideon M. Hart, "The 'Original' Thirteenth Amendment: The Misunderstood Titles of Nobility Amendment," *Marquette Law Review* 94 (2010): 313.

274. Trevor Burrus, "Sleep Well, President Trump—There Are no Emoluments under the Bed," *The Hill*, January 16, 2017, http://thehill.com/blogs/pundits-blog/the-administration/338153-slee p-well-president-trump-there-are-no-emoluments.

275. Natelson, "The Original Meaning of 'Emoluments,'" p. 55.

276. Jonathan Elliot, *The Debates in the Several State Conventions of the Adoption of the Federal Constitution*, vol. 3 (Virginia) [1827], Liberty Fund, http://oll.libertyfund.org/titles/1907#Elliot_1314-03_1019.

277. "Impeaching Donald J. Trump, President of the United States, of High Crimes and Misdemeanors," H. Res. 621, 115th Cong., November 15, 2017.

278. "Impeaching Donald J. Trump, President of the United States, of High Crimes and Misdemeanors," H. Res. 621, 115th Cong., November 15, 2017.

279. See, for example, David Frum, *Trumpocracy: The Corruption of the American Republic* (New York: Harper, 2018), ch. 4. These conflicts are unlikely to represent Foreign Emoluments Clause violations under the interpretation of that clause favored by professors Grewal and Natelson. Even so, they still raise issues of undue influence and potential corruption of the sort that concerned the Framers.

280. 26 U.S.C. § 6103(f). The committees so empowered are the House Ways and Means, the Senate Committee on Finance, and the Joint Committee on Taxation. See George K. Yin, "Congressional Authority to Obtain and Release Tax Returns," *Tax Notes*, February 20, 2017.

281. Darren Samuelsohn, "House Dems Press for Subpoenas on Trump Organization Operations," *Politico*, January 11, 2018.

282. Liz Stark, "Ben Sasse Blasts Trump's Twitter Behavior: 'This Isn't Normal,'" CNN.com, June 29, 2017, http://www.cnn.com/2017/06/29/politics/sasse-trump-twitter/index.html.

283. See Jasmine C. Lee and Kevin Quealy, "The 394 People, Places and Things Donald Trump Has Insulted on Twitter: A Complete List," https://www.nytimes.com/interactive/2016/01/28/upshot/donald-trump-twitter-insults.html?_r=0.

284. Carla Herreria, "Naval Ceremony Turns Political after Donald Trump Asks Crowd to Call Congress," Yahoo.com, July 22, 2017, https://www.yahoo.com/news/naval-ceremony-turns-political-donald-033738723.html; and Sophie Tatum, "Trump after 'Lock Her Up' Chant: Talk to Jeff Sessions," CNN.com, September 23, 2017, http://www.cnn.com/2017/09/22/politics/donald-trump-alabama-hillary-clinton/index.html.

285. Ramesh Ponnuru, "Trump's Tweets and Republicans," *NationalReview.com*, June 29, 2017, http://www.nationalreview.com/corner/449130/trumps-tweets-and-republicans.

286. Megan McArdle, "Trump Disgusts Republicans. What Are They Going to Do?" *Bloomberg.com*, August 17, 2017, https://www.bloomberg.com/view/articles/2017-08-17/trump-disgusts-republicans-what-are-they-going-to-do-about-it.

287. "Ranking Member Cohen to Introduce Articles of Impeachment against President Donald Trump after Comments on Charlottesville." The five articles Representative Cohen eventually introduced in November 2017 do not reference the Charlottesville incident, but include charges based on presidential speech "undermining the independence of the federal judiciary" and "undermining freedom of the press." "Impeaching Donald J. Trump, President of the United States, of High Crimes and Misdemeanors," H. Res. 621, 115th Cong., November 15, 2017.

288. Cristina Marcos, "House Democrat Unveils Articles of Impeachment against Trump, but Misses Chance to Force Vote," *The Hill*, October 11, 2017, http://thehill.com/homenews/house/354935-house-democrat-unveils-articles-of-impeachment-against-trump. Impeaching Donald John Trump, President of the United States, of High Misdemeanors, H. Res. 646,115th Cong., December 6, 2017.

289. Mike DeBonis, "House Votes to Kill Texas Lawmaker's Trump Impeachment Effort," *Washington Post*, December 6, 2017, https://www.washingtonpost.com/news/powerpost/wp/2017/12/06/house-democratic-leaders-oppose-texas-lawmakers-trump-impeachment-effort/?utm_term=.5d2d792b6017. A second attempt, brought by Representative Green in January 2018, garnered 66 votes. Cristina Marcos, "House Rejects Democratic Effort to Impeach Trump as Shutdown Looms," *The Hill*, January 19, 2018, http://thehill.com/blogs/floor-action/house/369730-house-rejects-democratic-effort-to-impeach-trump-as-shutdown-looms.

290. "Nixon Inquiry Report," p. 18.

291. "Nixon Inquiry Report," p. 21.

292. *Hinds' Precedents*, § 2346.

293. House Judiciary Committee, "Impeachment of G. Thomas Porteous, Jr.," p. 17.

294. United States Senate, "The Impeachment of Andrew Johnson (1868) President of the United States: Articles of Impeachment."
295. Stewart, *Impeached: the Trial of President Andrew Johnson and the Fight for Lincoln's Legacy*, p. 69.
296. Senator William Pitt Fessenden, a Republican "recusant," suggested it would deny the president "a right secured to every other citizen of the republic." Although Johnson's speeches were "a matter of deep regret and highly censurable," they could "receive no other punishment than public sentiment alone can inflict." Quoted in Rehnquist, *Grand Inquests*, pp. 241–42.
297. Benjamin F. Butler, *Autobiography and Personal Reminiscences of Major-General Benjamin F. Butler* (Boston: A. M. Thayer & Co., 1892), p. 926.
298. Jeffrey K. Tulis, *The Rhetorical Presidency* (Princeton: Princeton University Press, 1987), pp. 87–88.
299. "There must come a point" was Black's repeated refrain on questions of "substantiality." See, generally, Black, *Impeachment: A Handbook*; and Jane Chong, "To Impeach a President: Applying the Authoritative Guide from Charles Black," *Lawfare*, July 20, 2017, https://www.lawfareblog.com/impeach-president-applying -authoritative-guide-charles-black.
300. "Ranking Member Cohen to Introduce Articles of Impeachment against President Donald Trump After Comments on Charlottesville," press release, August 17, 2017, https://cohen. house.gov/media-center/press-releases/ranking-member -cohen-introduce-articles-impeachment-against-president.
301. Sanford Levinson, "Our Constitution Wasn't Built for Trump," *Democracy*, August 28, 2017, https://democracyjournal.org/ arguments/our-constitution-wasnt-built-for-trump/.
302. *Federalist* 69, in Carey and McClellan, eds., *The Federalist*, p. 361.
303. Representative Brad Sherman, "Re: Article of Impeachment Attached," June 20, 2017, https://sherman.house.gov/sites/ sherman.house.gov/files/Rep%2C%20Sherman%20-%20 Impeachment%20Dear%20Colleague%20-%20June%202017.pdf.
304. Daniel J. Hemel and Eric A. Posner, "Presidential Obstruction of Justice," July 22, 2017, p. 23, https://papers.ssrn.com/sol3/papers. cfm?abstract_id=3004876.
305. Hemel and Posner, "Presidential Obstruction of Justice," p. 25.

306. Committee on the Judiciary, House of Representatives, "Impeachment of William Jefferson Clinton, President of the United States," 105th Congress, December 16, 1998, Report 105-830, pp. 244–57.

307. See, for example, Statement of Senator Biden, 145 Cong. Rec. § 1480: "impeachment has no place in our system of constitutional democracy except as an extreme measure—reserved for breaches of the public trust by a President who so violates his official duties, misuses his official powers or places our system of government at such risk that our constitutional government is put in immediate danger by his continuing to serve out the term to which the people of the United States elected him."

308. Articles of Impeachment introduced in November 2017 by Representative Cohen also included obstruction of justice charges. See "Impeaching Donald J. Trump, President of the United States, of High Crimes and Misdemeanors," H. Res. 621, 115th Cong., November 15, 2017, https://www.congress.gov/bill/115th-congress/house-resolution/621?q=%7B%22search%22%3A%5B%22impeachment%22%5D%7D&r=3.

309. Representative Brad Sherman, "Re: Article of Impeachment Attached."

310. See, for example, Alan Dershowitz, "History, Precedent and James Comey's Opening Statement Show that Trump Did Not Obstruct Justice," *Washington Examiner*, June 8, 2017, http://www.washingtonexaminer.com/alan-dershowitz-history-precedent-and-james-comeys-opening-statement-show-that-trump-did-not-obstruct-justice/article/2625318; and John Yoo and David Marston, "No Case for Obstruction from Hyper-hyped Comey Hearing," *Philadelphia Inquirer*, June 11, 2017, http://www.philly.com/philly/opinion/commentary/no-case-for-obstruction-from-hyper-hyped-comey-hearing-20170609.html?mobi=true.

311. Greg Weiner, Twitter, June 8, 2017, 11:03 a.m., https://twitter.com/gregweiner1/status/872831374599876608.

312. House Judiciary Committee, "Impeachment of Richard M. Nixon, President of the United States," 93rd Cong., 2d sess., August 20, 1974, Report No. 93-1305, p. 136. The House Judiciary Committee report in the Clinton impeachment also emphasized this point: "the actions of President Clinton do not have to rise to the level

of violating the federal statute regarding obstruction of justice in order to justify impeachment." Clinton Report, p. 64.

313. "The Trump Lawyers' Confidential Memo to Mueller, Explained," *New York Times*, June 2, 2018, https://www.nytimes.com/interactive/2018/06/02/us/politics/trump-legal-documents.html.

314. See, for example, Barry H. Burke, Noah Bookbinder, and Norman L. Eisen, "Presidential Obstruction of Justice: the Case of Donald J. Trump," Brookings Institution, October 10, 2017, pp. 76–77 (citing case law showing lawful conduct ruled to be obstruction of justice), https://www.brookings.edu/wp-content/uploads/2017/10/presidential-obstruction-of-justice-the-case-of-donald-j-trump-final.pdf.

315. For a contrary view, see Josh Blackman, "Obstruction of Justice and the Presidency: Part III," *Lawfare*, December 18, 2017, https://www.lawfareblog.com/obstruction-justice-and-presidency-part-iii.

316. See Judiciary Committee Report, "Impeachment of Richard M. Nixon," p. 135, listing "the firing of Cox" among the "pattern of undisputed acts" supporting impeachment for obstruction of justice.

317. Carol D. Leonnig, Ashley Parker, Rosalind S. Helderman, and Tom Hamburger, "Trump Team Seeks to Control, Block Mueller's Russia Investigation," *Washington Post*, July 21, 2017, https://www.washingtonpost.com/politics/trumps-lawyers-seek-to-undercut-muellers-russia-investigation/2017/07/20/232ebf2c-6d71-11e7-b9e2-2056e768a7e5_story.html?utm_term=.619f3c4a60af.

318. Donald J. Trump, Twitter, July 22, 2017, 6:35 a.m., https://twitter.com/realdonaldtrump/status/888724194820857857.

319. "Unlimited, with the exception stated." *Ex parte Garland*, 71 U.S. 333, 380 (1866).

320. Sanford Levinson, *An Argument Open to All* (New Haven: Yale University Press, 2015), p. 281.

321. McClellan and Bradford, eds., *Elliot's Debates*, p. 612.

322. Jonathan Elliot, *The Debates in the Several State Conventions of the Adoption of the Federal Constitution*, vol. 2 (Massachusetts, Connecticut, New Hampshire, New York, Pennsylvania, Maryland) [1827], Liberty Fund, http://oll.libertyfund.org/titles/1906#Elliot_1314-02_1579.

323. Jonathan Elliot, *The Debates in the Several State Conventions of the Adoption of the Federal Constitution*, vol. 3 (Virginia) [1827], Liberty

Fund, http://oll.libertyfund.org/titles/elliot-the-debates-in-the
-several-state-conventions-vol-3#Elliot_1314-03_1047.

324. Jeffrey Crouch, *The Presidential Pardon Power* (Lawrence, KS:
University of Kansas Press, 2009), pp. 101–7, 112–17.

325. Frank O. Bowman, "Comparing Apples (Gala) with Apples (Fuji):
The Arpaio & Marc Rich Pardons," ImpeachableOffenses.net,
August 28, 2017, https://impeachableoffenses.net/2017/08/28/
comparing-apples-gala-with-apples-fuji-the-arpaio-marc-rich
-pardons/.

326. Federal officials can be—and have been—impeached even after
leaving office. In 1876, the House impeached Secretary of War
William W. Belknap despite his having resigned two hours
before the vote. The Senate held the trial despite the objection
of Belknap's counsel that Belknap was no longer a federal officer.
Cole and Garvey, *Impeachment and Removal*, CRS Report no.
R44260, p. 16. See also Brian C. Kalt, "The Constitutional Case
for the Impeachability of Former Federal Officials," *Texas Review
of Law and Politics* 6 (2001–2002): 13–135.

327. Andrew Rudalevige, "Why Trump's Pardon of Joe Arpaio Isn't
Like Most Presidential Pardons," *Washington Post*, August 26,
2017, https://www.washingtonpost.com/news/monkey-cage/
wp/2017/08/26/why-trumps-pardon-of-joe-arpaio-isnt-like
-most-presidential-pardons/?utm_term=.4bbfcced8781. For a look
at Arpaio's record, see Nathan J. Robinson, "Wait, Do People
Actually Know Just How Evil This Man Is?" *Current Affairs*, August
26, 2017, https://static.currentaffairs.org/2017/08/wait-do-people
-actually-know-just-how-evil-this-man-is.

328. *Federalist* 74, in Carey and McClellan, eds., *The Federalist*, p. 385.

329. "Impeaching Donald J. Trump, President of the United States,
of High Crimes and Misdemeanors," H. Res. 621, 115th Cong.,
November 15, 2017.

330. Frank Bowman, "Trump's Pardon of Joe Arpaio Is an Impeachable
Offense," *Slate.com*, August 26, 2017, http://www.slate.com/articles/
news_and_politics/jurisprudence/2017/08/trump_s_pardon_of_
joe_arpaio_is_an_impeachable_offense.html.

331. James Warren, "Nixon's Hoffa Pardon Has an Odor," *Chicago
Tribune*, April 8, 2001.

332. Robert Pear, "President Reagan Pardons 2 Ex-F.B.I. Officials
in 1970's Break-Ins," *New York Times*, April 16, 1981. One of

the officials Reagan pardoned was Mark Felt, who, it was later revealed, had been Watergate's "Deep Throat."

333. Robert Costa, "Trump Fixates on Pardons, Could Soon Give Reprieve to 63-year-old Woman after Meeting with Kim Kardashian," *Washington Post*, June 5, 2018, https://www. washingtonpost.com/politics/trump-fixates-on-pardons-could -soon-give-reprieve-to-63-year-old-woman-after-meeting-with -kim-kardashian/2018/06/05/37ac6cb6-683d-11e8-bbc5-dc9f3 634faoa_story.html.

334. "Nixon Inquiry Report," p. 24.

335. Mason, quoted in McClellan and Bradford, eds., *Elliot's Debates*, p. 572.

336. Alexander Hamilton and James Madison, *The Pacificus-Helvidius Debates of 1793–1794: Toward the Completion of the American Founding*, ed. and introduction by Morton J. Frisch (Indianapolis: Liberty Fund, 2007) p. 87.

337. Evan Osnos, "The Risk of Nuclear War with North Korea," *New Yorker*, September 18, 2017, https://www.newyorker.com/ magazine/2017/09/18/the-risk-of-nuclear-war-with-north-korea.

338. Jennifer Daskal, "Trump on North Korea: The Dangerous Impulse to Go It Alone," JustSecurity.org, April 18, 2017, https://www. justsecurity.org/40051/trump-north-korea-dangerous-impulse/.

339. Julia Manchester, "Trump on Attacking North Korea: 'We'll See,'" *The Hill*, September 3, 2017, http://thehill.com/homenews/ administration/349056-trump-well-see-if-the-us-attacks-north -korea.

340. Ken Klippenstein, "Leading Progressive Dem. Congressman: War with North Korea Is Grounds for Impeachment," *Alternet.org*, August 10, 2017, https://img.alternet.org/world/ war-north-korea-grounds-impeachment.

341. McClellan and Bradford, eds., *Elliot's Debates*, pp. 318–19.

342. Arthur Schlesinger, Jr., *The Imperial Presidency* (Boston: Houghton-Mifflin Co., 1973), p. ix.

343. "Nixon Judiciary Committee Report," p. 219.

344. See, generally, John Hart Ely, *War and Responsibility: Constitutional Lessons of Vietnam and Its Aftermath* (Princeton: Princeton University Press, 1993), ch. 5, pp. 98–105.

345. Seymour M. Hersh, "US Confirms Pre-1970s Raids on Cambodia," *New York Times*, July 17, 1973; and William Shawcross, *Sideshow:*

Kissinger, Nixon, and the Destruction of Cambodia (London: Fontana Paperbacks, 1980), p. 287.

346. "Nixon Judiciary Committee Report," p. 218. After the widely publicized ground incursion into Cambodia in 1970, Nixon announced his intention to continue bombing after U.S. troops were withdrawn. "However, the fact that we had been bombing Cambodia from March 1969 through April 1970 remained secret until 1973." Ely, *War and Responsibility*, p. 98.

347. Richard L. Madden, "Nixon Accepts a Cutoff," *New York Times*, July 1, 1973, http://www.nytimes.com/1973/07/01/archives/the-world-cambodia-bombing.html.

348. "Nixon Judiciary Committee Report," p. 217.

349. John Hart Ely, "The American War in Indochina, Part II: The Unconstitutionality of the War They Didn't Tell Us About," *Stanford Law Review* 42 (May 1990): 1146.

350. "Nixon Judiciary Committee Report," p. 219.

351. Black, *Impeachment: A Handbook*, p. 35.

352. *Federalist* 66, in Carey and McClellan, eds., *The Federalist*, p. 346.

353. Jonathan Elliot, *The Debates in the Several State Conventions of the Adoption of the Federal Constitution*, vol. 3 (Virginia) [1827], Liberty Fund, http://oll.libertyfund.org/titles/1907#Elliot_1314-03_1092.

354. *Federalist* 66, in Carey and McClellan, eds., *The Federalist*, p. 347.

355. Black, *Impeachment: A Handbook*, p. 44.

356. Expressing the sense of Congress that the use of offensive military force by a president without prior and clear authorization of an act of Congress constitutes an impeachable high crime and misdemeanor under Article II, Section 4 of the Constitution, see H. Con. Res. 107, 112th Cong., 2d sess., March 7, 2012, https://www.congress.gov/bill/112th-congress/house-concurrent-resolution/107/text.

357. "Restricting First Use of Nuclear Weapons Act of 2017," H.R. 669, 115th Cong., 1st sess., January 24, 2017; and "Preventing Preemptive War in North Korea Act of 2017," S. 2407, 115th Cong., 2d sess., October 31, 2017.

358. McClellan and Bradford, eds., *Elliot's Debates*, p. 573.

359. George Mason: "Some mode of displacing an unfit magistrate is rendered indispensable by the fallibility of those who choose, as well as by the corruptibility of the man chosen." James Madison: "thought it indispensable that some provision should be made

for defending the Community agst. the incapacity, negligence or perfidy of the chief Magistrate." Quoted in McClellan and Bradford, eds., *Elliot's Debates*, pp. 55, 317.

360. F. H. Buckley, *The Once and Future King: The Rise of Crown Government in America* (New York: Encounter Books, 2014), p. 290.

361. See, for example, Robert J. Samuelson, "Are We on the Road to Impeachment?," *Washington Post*, May 28, 2017 (describing impeachment as "reversing elections," "overturn[ing] the results of an election," and "damaging the integrity of the ballot"), https:// www.washingtonpost.com/opinions/the-path-to-impeachment -is-an-uneasy-one/2017/05/28/79718632-4222-11e7-8c25-44d09ff5 a4a8_story.html?utm_term=.af7c97626769; and "The I Word: Let's All Take a Breath," *Manchester Union-Leader* (Manchester, NH), May 22, 2017 ("hysterical critics of President Donald Trump are leaping to impeachment as a way to reverse an election"), http:// www.unionleader.com/editorial/The-I-Word-Lets-all-take-a -breath-05232017.

362. "On Impeaching Trump," *Los Angeles Times*, June 10, 2017, http:// www.latimes.com/opinion/editorials/la-ed-impeach-trump -20170610-story.html.

363. Patrick J. Buchanan, "The Impeach-Trump Conspiracy," *RealClearPolitics*, June 9, 2017, https://www.realclearpolitics.com/ articles/2017/06/09/the_impeach-trump_conspiracy_134146. html. For other examples, see Gene Healy, "Crying 'Coup,' Red and Blue," *Cato@Liberty*, June 15, 2017, https://www.cato.org/blog/ crying-coup-red-blue.

364. See, for example, "Impeachment; Excerpts from the House's Final Debate on Impeaching President Clinton," *New York Times*, December 20, 1998; and Ronald Dworkin, "A Kind of Coup," *New York Review of Books*, January 14, 1999.

365. Black, *Impeachment: A Handbook*, p. 2.

366. Statement of Laurence H. Tribe, "Background and History of Impeachment."

367. Dworkin, "A Kind of Coup." See also Berger, *Impeachment: The Constitutional Problems*, p. 91 ("Removal of the President must generate shock waves that can rock the very foundations of government"); and Sunstein, "Impeaching the President," p. 312 ("destabilizing in a way that threatens to punish the Nation as much as, or perhaps far more than, the President himself").

368. Before the Twelfth Amendment, removing the president would replace him with his principal electoral opponent; before the Twenty-fifth Amendment, the Constitution lacked a means for filling midterm vacancies in the vice presidency. Had Richard Nixon not been able to nominate Gerald Ford under Section 2 of the Twenty-fifth Amendment, his replacement would have been Speaker of the House Carl Albert, a Democrat. Thanks to that provision, "Congress was able to conduct the impeachment in the months that followed with the knowledge that it could not be charged with attempting to turn over control of the executive to the Democrats by installing the House Speaker as President." John D. Feerick, "Presidential Succession and Inability: Before and After the Twenty-Fifth Amendment," *Fordham Law Review* 79 (2010): 933.

369. Merriam-Webster's Dictionary defines "coup d'état" as "a sudden decisive exercise of force in politics; especially: the violent overthrow or alteration of an existing government by a small group," https://www.merriam-webster.com/dictionary/coup%20 d'%C3%A9tat.

370. Richard A. Posner, "Dworkin, Polemics, and the Clinton Impeachment Controversy," *Northwestern University Law Review* 94 (2000): 1030.

371. Posner, *Affair of State*, p. 263.

372. *Federalist* 65, in Carey and McClellan, eds., *The Federalist*, p. 339.

373. *Federalist* 66, in Carey and McClellan, eds., *The Federalist*, p. 343.

374. McClellan and Bradford, eds., *Elliot's Debates*, p. 318.

375. Jonathan Elliot, *The Debates in the Several State Conventions of the Adoption of the Federal Constitution*, vol. 4 (North and South Carolina, Resolutions, Tariffs, Banks, Debt)[1827], Liberty Fund, http://oll.libertyfund.org/titles/1908#Elliot_1314-04_156.

376. The better-known of these episodes was the Senate's 1834 censure of Andrew Jackson for "assum[ing] upon himself authority and power not conferred by the Constitution" during the fight over the Second Bank of the United States, expunged from the Senate records in 1837. Others include James Buchanan, censured by the House in 1860 for issuing military contracts on a partisan basis. See Jane A. Hudiburg and Christopher M. Davis, *Resolutions to Censure the President: Procedure and History*, CRS Report no. R45087 (Washington: Congressional Research Service, 2018).

377. See also Hoffer and Hull, *Impeachment in America: 1635–1805*, p. 4. (In 17th-century England, the House of Lords "tried very few of the cases brought to them and convicted only one in twenty of those impeached. On many occasions the Commons did not even prosecute—the impeachment itself was sufficient warning or inconvenience to the accused.")

378. One such case, Keith Whittington suggests, was the impeachment of Supreme Court Justice Samuel Chase. "The willingness of the House to impeach was sufficient to signal to the judiciary, still largely controlled by Federalist appointees, that partisanship in the conduct of their official duties would not be tolerated, and federal judges rapidly and obviously moved to a more neutral position relative to 'political' conflicts." Keith E. Whittington, *Constitutional Construction: Divided Powers and Constitutional Meaning* (Cambridge: Harvard University Press: 1999), p. 41.

379. Keith Whittington, "What Is the Impeachment Power For?," *Law and Liberty*, May 22, 2017, http://www.libertylawsite. org/2017/05/22/what-is-the-impeachment-power-for/.

380. See Ezra Klein, "The Case for Normalizing Impeachment," *Vox*, December 6, 2017, https://www.vox.com/2017/11/30/16517022/ impeachment-donald-trump. ("We have created a political culture in which firing our national executive is viewed as a crisis rather than as a difficult but occasionally necessary act.")

381. A 2006 study surveying some 375 employment contracts for CEOs at large public companies found that the overwhelming majority of such contracts included "moral turpitude" or "gross misconduct" clauses. Stewart J. Schwartz and Randall S. Thomas, "An Empirical Analysis of CEO Employment Contracts: What Do Top Executives Bargain For?" *Washington & Lee Law Review* 63 (2006): 248–49. A similar survey of college football-coach employment contracts finds that more than 65 percent contain a termination clause for "unprofessional conduct." Randall S. Thomas and R. Lawrence Van Horn, "Are College Presidents Like Football Coaches? Evidence from Their Employment Contracts," *Arizona Law Review* 58 (2016): 946.

About the Author

Gene Healy is a vice president at the Cato Institute. His research interests include executive power and the role of the presidency as well as federalism and overcriminalization. He is the author of *False Idol: Barack Obama and the Continuing Cult of the Presidency* and *The Cult of the Presidency: America's Dangerous Devotion to Executive Power*; and is editor of *Go Directly to Jail: The Criminalization of Almost Everything*.

His work has been published in the *Los Angeles Times*, the *New York Times*, the *Chicago Tribune*, the *Legal Times*, and elsewhere.

Healy holds a BA from Georgetown University and a JD from the University of Chicago Law School.

 @GeneHealy
#CatoBooks

ABOUT THE CATO INSTITUTE

Founded in 1977, the Cato Institute is a public policy research foundation dedicated to broadening the parameters of policy debate to allow consideration of more options that are consistent with the principles of limited government, individual liberty, and peace. To that end, the Institute strives to achieve greater involvement of the intelligent, concerned lay public in questions of policy and the proper role of government.

The Institute is named for Cato's Letters, libertarian pamphlets that were widely read in the American Colonies in the early 18th century and played a major role in laying the philosophical foundation for the American Revolution.

Despite the achievement of the nation's Founders, today virtually no aspect of life is free from government encroachment. A pervasive intolerance for individual rights is shown by government's arbitrary intrusions into private economic transactions and its disregard for civil liberties. And while freedom around the globe has notably increased in the past several decades, many countries have moved in the opposite direction, and most governments still do not respect or safeguard the wide range of civil and economic liberties.

To address those issues, the Cato Institute undertakes an extensive publications program on the complete spectrum of policy issues. Books, monographs, and shorter studies are commissioned to examine the federal budget, Social Security, regulation, military spending, international trade, and myriad other issues. Major policy conferences are held through-out the year, from which papers are published thrice yearly in the Cato Journal. The Institute also publishes the quarterly magazine Regulation.

In order to maintain its independence, the Cato Institute accepts no government funding. Contributions are received from foundations, corporations, and individuals, and other revenue is generated from the sale of publications. The Institute is a non-profit, tax-exempt, educational foundation under Section 501(c)3 of the Internal Revenue Code.

Cato Institute
1000 Massachusetts Ave., N.W.
Washington, D.C. 20001
www.cato.org

CPSIA information can be obtained
at www.ICGtesting.com
Printed in the USA
FSHW022308120119
54906FS